# THE AUTHORS

Dr. Stanley I. Stuber, a native of Maine and a graduate of Bates College, studied theology at Colgate Rochester Divinity School. Now a Baptist clergyman, he has traveled widely in behalf of improved racial understanding, and has attended sessions of the United Nations as an Official Observer. For many years he has served as chairman of various committees of the National Council of Churches of Christ in the USA. Long experience in both public relations and communications contributed to his success as first National Director of the "Religion in American Life" program. As an authority on Roman Catholic relationships, Dr. Stuber wrote *Primer on Roman Catholicism for Protestants,* one of his eleven published books. At the invitation of Cardinal Bea, President of the Secretariat for Promoting Christian Unity, he was present at all four sessions of the Second Vatican Council, and has written and lectured widely on its work.

Dr. Claud D. Nelson, an ordained minister of the Methodist Church, is a graduate of Hendrix College, and also of Oxford University, which he attended as a Rhodes Scholar from Arkansas. For more than thirty years, he was active in the Y.M.C.A. in Russia, Germany, Switzerland, and Italy, and during both World Wars he worked for the welfare of prisoners of war. At home between wars, he continued his association with the "Y" in the South, where he pioneered in racial and industrial relations. Since 1959 he has been Consultant on Religious Liberty for the National Conference of Christians and Jews. During Vatican II, Dr. Nelson was stationed in Rome, whence he reported on the Council for the Religious News Service. His interest in ecumenism has been given expression in three books: *The Vatican Council and All Christians* (1962), *Religion and Society: The Ecumenical Impact* (1966), and the present volume.

# IMPLEMENTING VATICAN II IN YOUR COMMUNITY

DIALOGUE AND ACTION MANUAL
BASED ON THE SIXTEEN DOCUMENTS
OF THE SECOND VATICAN COUNCIL

By Stanley I. Stuber
and Claud D. Nelson

Foreword by
Father Walter M. Abbott, S.J.

*From*
*Lou Stuber Spitzer*

GUILD PRESS · NEW YORK
ASSOCIATION PRESS

*Designed and produced by Artists and Writers Press, Inc.*
*Printed in the U.S.A. by Western Printing and Lithographing Co.*
*Library of Congress Catalogue Number: 67–10935*

*Dedicated to*
# POPE PAUL VI
*Christian Statesman*

# CALL TO ECUMENICAL DIALOGUE
# AND ACTION

"Pope Paul VI has called for the prompt application of the teachings of the Council in the life of the Church. Men and women of good will everywhere can applaud his determination and can pray that the gifts of the Holy Spirit will continue to be poured upon the Church which He leads."

> —Bishop Reuben H. Mueller, President of the National Council of the Churches of Christ in the U.S.A., in an introductory note to *The Documents of Vatican II.*

"It was a sense of continuity which inspired the saying, 'The king is dead; long live the king.' A similar sense would justify the statement, 'The Council is over; the Council has just begun.'"

> —Lawrence Cardinal Shehan, Archbishop of Baltimore, in the Introduction to *The Documents of Vatican II.*

"The test of the Decree will be found in what now happens in local communities. It is there that the full meaning of it will be explored and discovered. The great thing to be desired at this juncture is that Christian congregations of every name begin to move forward in both dialogue and concrete measures of cooperation such as the Decree recommends. The inherited patterns of separateness and suspicion will not be overcome easily, but Vatican Council II is a challenge to all Christians to follow the more excellent way."

> —Dr. Samuel McCrea Cavert, former General Secretary of the National Council of Churches, in Response to the Decree on Ecumenism in *The Documents of Vatican II.*

# Table of Contents

## Part Four

# IMPLEMENTATION: OF CONSCIENCE AND RENEWAL

## Epilogue

# THE CHALLENGE OF THE "DEVELOPMENT OF DOCTRINE"

## Appendices

# Foreword

By Walter M. Abbott, S.J.

Pope John XXIII had great hopes and expectations when he convoked an Ecumenical Council and named it Vatican II. It has often been said that he wanted to update the Roman Catholic Church, in order to prepare the way for Christian unity, and that he wanted to make the Roman Catholic Church understandable and relevant for people of the twentieth century. Actually, he wanted to do much more. He wanted everything possible done to help the Christian message reach all men.

The opening Message to Humanity of Vatican II, issued by Pope John and all the Council Fathers, made this great purpose quite clear. It declared: "In this assembly, under the guidance of the Holy Spirit, we wish to inquire how we ought to renew ourselves, so that we may be found increasingly faithful to the gospel of Christ. We shall take pains so to present to the men of this age God's truth in its integrity and purity that they may understand it and gladly assent to it."

If Vatican II succeeded in its purpose, its work should be helpful to all Christians and to all mankind. Some have called Vatican II the most important religious event of the twentieth century. Others have exposed its shortcomings and flaws. Generally, religious leaders and critics agree that much of what Vatican II produced is important and helpful for Christianity and for all men. It is in this spirit that Dr. Stuber and Dr. Nelson have produced their book.

It is evident that these two Protestant scholars regard much of Vatican II as belonging to them and to all Christians; they clearly regard much of what Vatican II produced as authentic Christian belief and planning. Thus, they have forthrightly called their book *Implementing Vatican II in Your Community*. This is the kind of response Pope

John hoped for. The appearance of this book is striking evidence that his hopes are being realized.

The book is remarkable for several reasons. It is the first dialogue and action manual on the sixteen documents of Vatican II. It is the first full-scale treatment of a program for implementation of Vatican II. It is the first book to bring such a full-scale program to the parish or community level. And, no doubt most remarkable of all for the Catholic beholder, this ground-breaking book is the work of two Protestants.

However well or poorly this book were done, it would, by the very nature of the case, be used far and wide. The hopes of people everywhere have been aroused by Pope John, by Vatican II, and by the responses of leading churchmen throughout the world. The people will reach for this book. Fortunately, they will not be disappointed. It is the work of experts, and it is so well done that it is destined to be serviceable for many years to come.

The plan of the book is quite simple. There is a rigorously honest summary of Vatican II's work on a topic; then comes a factual survey of Protestant and Eastern Orthodox views on that topic; the authors make an assessment of the differences and discuss what is required for working the differences out; finally there are questions for dialogue and suggestions for action.

If the good work of Vatican II is going to bear its fruit, it is vital, of course, that men and women throughout our communities engage in the dialogue and action outlined by this book. The Roman Catholic Church's effort of renewal in Vatican II, that Christian unity might be promoted and that the Christian message might reach the world more effectively, has brought many other Christian leaders to pray and work more ardently for Christian unity and for the Christian mission. But we know from history that earlier attempts at Christian unity failed because the people did not follow their leaders, and we see how often people go their way apparently unconcerned about their role in the Christian mission because they have not become involved.

If Franziskus Cardinal Koenig, Archbishop of Vienna, and others are right in holding that through Vatican II the Roman Catholic Church has its last great chance to reach the world with the message of Christ, then Catholics have a serious obligation to study the work of Vatican II and to seek how they can share in its implementation. If Vatican II has been important for Christianity, all Christians should make use of the good they discern in what Vatican II produced.

As the four years of the Council's work unfolded, the press and radio of the world gave attention and comment to the bishops' efforts to put forth true Christian views on the Bible, worship, ecumenism, the role of the people, bishops, priests, religious brothers and sisters in the Church, the use of communications media, education, religious freedom, missionary activity, attitudes toward Jews and other non-Christians, the problems of the modern world. Even before it was all over, leaders of various churches had manifested appreciation and enthusiasm for the efforts of the Council Fathers. Official high-level dialogues and programs of action were initiated. But it will all come to little or nothing if the people do not continue to manifest interest, take an active part, and thereby assure implementation of the truly Christian goals clarified by Vatican II. They need this kind of book to rekindle their interest and to guide them.

The book makes an important contribution to the dialogue of the post-conciliar era because its Protestant authorship reminds Roman Catholics that materials for the dialogue cannot be completely from Catholic sources. The Vatican II Decree on Ecumenism instructs Catholics that study is "absolutely required" for understanding "the outlook of our separated brethren," and that it should be pursued "with fidelity to truth and in a spirit of good will." The Decree states that Catholics need to acquire "a more adequate understanding of the distinctive doctrines . . . history, spiritual and liturgical life, religious psychology and cultural background" of the "separated brethren." Obviously, therefore, Catholics must study the best materials produced by these brethren themselves—just as Protestants and Orthodox will have to study competent Catholic writings for their knowledge of Catholic beliefs and practices. This objective, factual book by Dr. Stuber and Dr. Nelson is a bridge leading to the highway of the two-way traffic of the future.

Those who use this book will have a good model of the frankness and honesty that are essential elements in the dialogue. The authors' earlier books and articles have given them authority and stature in the ecumenical movement.

Their names immediately commend their work to Protestants. Catholics should know that Dr. Stuber, a Baptist, was an official guest-observer at Vatican II; he was invited to the Council by Augustin Cardinal Bea, president of the Secretariat for Promoting Christian Unity. Dr. Nelson, a Methodist, was official Religious News Service correspondent at Vatican II; he was sent by the National Conference of Christians and Jews.

Dr. Stuber and Dr. Nelson were quite right in discerning that more than dialogue was needed in our present era. They have wisely provided at the end of each chapter not only questions to stimulate dialogue but guidelines for action. In the two-way flow of conversation and action, it is right, of course, that ideas should come from both Protestants and Catholics. Not everyone will agree with every idea or recommendation in this book. How could it be otherwise? The reader should follow the example of the authors' honesty and frankness; he should be equally honest and frank in his appraisal of their assessments, questions, and suggestions for action. The users of this book will be intelligent enough, surely, to agree to disagree, and to move ahead together with what they see to be genuinely good and productive ideas.

This is more than a book to be read. It should be used by groups of Catholic, Protestant, and Orthodox people working together, on a regular schedule, over a period of, say, from September to June, meeting twice a month. An average or manageable group would be not more than twelve or fifteen people.

In many cases, more than twelve or fifteen people will want to follow the program. The whole group, even as many as a hundred, can meet in a church library or hall for a presentation and response by a Catholic and Protestant (or Orthodox) spokesman on the document to be discussed for the evening. Then the group can break up into the desired smaller groups, perhaps in adjacent school classrooms, to discuss questions raised by the speakers. After forty-five or fifty minutes, all can return to the assembly hall, where the proceedings of each group can be reported by a recording secretary, and questions can be directed to a panel of resource people (clergymen and others of the community who are specially qualified by their studies or occupations).

However the study is arranged, the focus should be not

on what divides the churches but on what they have in common—including the problems all Christians have in common in these times. It will quickly be seen that agreement and disagreement cut across denominational lines. The discussion will readily turn to opportunities for joint witness in the community.

The discussion procedure Dr. Stuber and Dr. Nelson have suggested in this book is a very natural one. I can say from experience it is one that works. A group I am acquainted with in Pelham, N. Y., spent three evenings in this kind of study of the documents of Vatican II and then formed a steering committee, made up of laymen from the participating churches, to implement the various ideas that had been produced and to promote more ways of praying, studying, and working together. A small group of women began the project. It quickly grew to include their husbands and other couples, with the approval and encouragement of their clergy.

One member of this group, Mrs. Harry McCallion, offers these suggestions to persons who want to start their own dialogue group: Look for persons well-grounded in their own faith; tactful, considerate persons who will not dominate or impose their viewpoints on others; persons involved in civic interests and responsibilities, such as members of the local League of Women Voters, local school boards, or community Human Relations Committees. Be open to all ideas and suggestions, whether you agree with them or not; be willing to learn and to change; help to distinguish facts from opinion. Your example in these matters will encourage others to do the same. Priests or ministers should be consulted to clear up any difficulties.

There is one difficulty that I can perhaps take care of right here. What authority, it will be asked, do the Council documents have? To what extent are Catholics bound by the Vatican II decrees? Pope Paul VI handled the matter in one of his Wednesday afternoon general audiences a little over a month after the conclusion of Vatican II. He said, on January 12, 1966:

> "Some ask what authority—what theological qualification—the Council has attached to its teachings, knowing that it has avoided pronouncing solemn dogmatic definitions backed by the Church's infallible teaching authority. The answer is familiar to those

who remember the conciliar declaration of March 6, 1964, repeated on November 16, 1964.[1] In view of the pastoral character of the Council, it has avoided pronouncing in an extraordinary way dogmas carrying the note of infallibility. Nevertheless, its teachings carry the weight of the supreme teaching authority. This ordinary teaching authority, so evidently authentic, must be received docilely and sincerely by all the faithful in accordance with the intentions of the Council regarding the nature and purpose of each of the documents."

Many sections of the Vatican II documents present doctrine; some describe historical developments or current situations; others prescribe discipline or regulate practices. Anyone who compares Articles 2, 4, and 10 in the Decree on Ecumenism can see the differences between doctrinal, historical, and disciplinary sections of the document. Obviously, where the text of a document sounds very much like the Apostles' Creed or the Nicene Creed, one is in an area of sacred doctrine that has remained unchanged and will always remain unchanged. Matters of discipline or practice have varied over the centuries, and there could be further changes. In fact, there have been changes within the documents of Vatican II concerning matters of discipline or practice. Compare, for example, the Decree on the Instruments of Social Communication (promulgated December 4, 1963) with the Decree on Ecumenism (November 21, 1964) and the Decree on the Missionary Activity of the Church (December 7, 1965). On a number of points, in my opinion, the Council Fathers effectively repealed the earlier document in the two later documents. In other words, within the documents of Vatican II there is evidence of progress in thinking, evidence of a development of ideas.

This book continues the ecumenical publishing venture begun with *The Documents of Vatican II*. It is the product of Catholic and Protestant publishing houses. The Protestant authors of this volume neither teach Catholic doctrine nor attack it polemically, and therefore the book may be used by Catholics without any special permission. In fact, the book performs a valuable service for Catholics, not

[1] The declaration that Pope Paul refers to may be found in *The Documents of Vatican II*, pp. 97-98.

only by providing the surveys of Protestant and Orthodox views, but also by keeping the reader informed about relevant developments in the World Council of Churches, the Consultation on Church Union in the United States, and other important ecumenical movements. The authors frequently cite useful comments by other experts: e.g., on the whole question of the Jews and Christianity, from various journals, speeches, and conferences, such as the Conference on the Main Theological Issues of Vatican II held at the University of Notre Dame in the spring of 1966.

In this book, therefore, a constantly stimulating and informative companion is available for all who wish to cover the ground of Vatican II. It is an excellent companion to *The Documents of Vatican II*.

WALTER M. ABBOTT, S.J.

# Introduction

WHILE certain publishing houses associated with the Roman Catholic Church have, during and since Vatican II, printed several study booklets dealing with specific documents of the Council, no study manual has yet dealt with all of the sixteen documents as a whole. This manual does. Moreover, prepared by two authors (a Methodist and a Baptist) who were closely identified with all four sessions of the Council, it is constructed in such a way as to be used by members of both Roman Catholic and Protestant-Orthodox churches. In other words, it is a truly *ecumenical* product and can be viewed either by Catholics or Protestants separately or by the two together in dialogue. It is another indication of the distance we have traveled in ecumenical relations.

Although basic information is absolutely essential to ecumenical understanding, dialogue is not enough. We need far more action of an ecumenical nature. This manual is designed specifically to encourage and to promote action. Thus the manual is weighted somewhat on the side of doing. It carefully explains the nature of the documents in order that directed and creative talk may culminate in positive, meaningful, and mutually helpful ecumenical action. Each chapter is divided into five sections: a brief introduction, a summary or digest of the document under consideration, the Protestant-Orthodox position in regard to the document, questions for discussion, and suggestions for ecumenical action.

While the Second Vatican Council made exciting ecclesiastical history, and changed both the external face of the Roman Catholic Church and its internal spirit, it is generally considered now that its greatest contribution will be related to the implementation of its official Constitutions, Decrees, and Declarations, in local communities around the world. This book is designed as a study and action manual, especially for concerned Catholic and Protestant laymen, to be used by them on the local level in many practical ways.

Laymen must know, if they are going to take intelligent action, just how far the Second Vatican Council went in ecumenical relations and possibilities. They ought to know, for example, what is contained in the historic Decree on Ecumenism and exactly how it affects Protestant-Roman Catholic relations. This book therefore gives in simple summary fashion the new developments in ecumenical relations, as well as the limitations and boundaries established by the Council. Every pastor, priest, Sunday School teacher, church executive, and active church member should know precisely how far the Church can go locally in such matters as are considered by the Constitutions, Decrees, and Declarations of the Second Vatican Council. This book, in a practical way, will serve not only for ecumenical discussion but also for specific ecumenical action—and the latter is all-important.

When it comes to the continuing dialogue it will be extremely helpful if all Christians know, at least in capsule form, what is contained in the documents of the Council pertaining to better Christian relationships. Because the new liturgy has several features of special concern to Protestants, these are outlined and supported by pertinent questions. The same is done with the new rules in regard to the organization of the hierarchy, the new ecumenical guidelines, the new position in regard to the Word of God, the new pronouncements in relation to non-Christians (and to the Jews in particular), the new declaration in the area of religious freedom, and in regard to the position the Roman Catholic Church now takes respecting Christian education.

The sections on ecumenical action indicate, on the basis of the new positions taken by the Council, how Catholics and Protestants can, and should, work together as Christian people and as members together of the mystical Church of Christ. Emphasis is placed upon the Church in the modern world. Practical aspects of how to utilize material for the ecumenical dialogue are developed.

This book, while directed chiefly toward laymen, has in it a rather large quantity of basic theology. It contains theological positions now taken by the Roman Catholic Church; it also indicates why non-Catholics can accept them, or why they must disagree with them. The authors of the book, who are both experienced in this whole area of ecumenical relations, feel at this stage in church unity development that the open spirit, based upon factual statements and mutual understanding, is the best foundation for realistic dialogue.

Both of the authors are aware of the fact that the Council has made just about all books, pamphlets, and mimeograph material dealing with Roman Catholic-Protestant relations, dated. This book, therefore, represents an attempt to bring Christians up-to-date in respect to the new positions taken by the Roman Catholic Church and to provide guidelines for all those who want to go, as far as it is now possible, up the road of united Christian action for the sake of Christ in the modern world.

Excerpts from the Constitutions, Declarations, and Decrees of the Ecumenical Council are taken from *The Documents of Vatican II*, edited by Walter M. Abbott, S.J., and published by Herder and Herder and Association Press; the book is also available in a paperback edition which has been published by America Press, Guild Press, and Association Press.

STANLEY I. STUBER
CLAUD D. NELSON

*New York City*
*Jan. 1, 1967*

# PART ONE

# Implementation: Within the Church

"The Second Vatican Council is, without doubt, a 'challenge' for Catholic theology, since it sets up new tasks, provides it with a stronger dynamic and gives a wider space for freedom of movement."

> —DR. KARL RAHNER, S.J., at the International Conference on the Main Theological Issues of Vatican II at the University of Notre Dame.

> "The liturgy is thus the outstanding means by which the faithful can express in their lives, and manifest to others, the mystery of Christ and the real nature of the true Church." (The Constitution on the Sacred Liturgy, Art. 2.)

## CHAPTER I

# The Living Altar

## INTRODUCTION

In the past the Roman Catholic Church has been accused, and rightly so, of having its worship in a strange tongue, of encouraging vain repetitions, and of placing more trust in form than in spirit. Now, with the Constitution on the Sacred Liturgy (*Sacrosanctum Concilium*), promulgated at the Second Vatican Council on December 4, 1963, by Pope Paul VI, this can no longer be said. In the revision of its liturgy the Roman Catholic Church has cut away useless forms and repetitions and has permitted the faithful in their own native language to enter into the worship of the Church as active participants and not as mere observers. This, and its implications, has caused in each parish a process of reform and renewal which goes to the very heart of the gospel. There are also ecumenical overtones in the new liturgy which are a real challenge to non-Catholics and in particular to Protestants.

## I. SUMMARY OF THE NEW LITURGY

The Constitution on the Sacred Liturgy is so revolu-tionary, and so essential to an understanding of what is happening within the whole ecumenical movement, that it is important to know what it actually says. Therefore we present here a summary of the Constition, giving, in its own words when it is deemed necessary, the substance of the document.

It begins with a paragraph giving the basic aims of the Council, followed by a second paragraph on the nature of the liturgy reform.

> "It is the goal of this most sacred Council to intensify the daily growth of Catholics in Christian living; to make more responsive to the requirements of our times those Church observances which are open to adaptation; to nurture whatever can contribute to the unity of all who believe in Christ; and to strengthen those aspects of the Church which can help summon all of mankind into her embrace. Hence the Council has special reasons for judging it a duty to provide for the renewal and fostering of the liturgy." (Art. 1.)

In the Introduction it is also noted that the Council recognizes that the Church holds all lawfully acknowledged rites to be of equal right and dignity; and that it wishes to preserve them in the future and to foster them in every way. Then it emphasizes the fact that the Council desires, when necessary, that the rites be revised carefully "in the light of sound tradition," and that they be given new vigor to meet the circumstances and needs of modern times.

Chapter I deals with general principles for the restoration and promotion of the sacred liturgy.

Under Section I the nature of the sacred liturgy and its importance in the Church's life are stressed. This section points out that the wonderful works of God among the people of the Old Testament were but a prelude to the work of Christ in redeeming mankind and giving perfect glory to God. And just as God sent his Son, so he also sent his apostles. It proceeds to recall the day of Pentecost "when the Church appeared before the world" and when those who received the word of Peter were baptized. In all this the work of the Holy Spirit is noted.

Not only the Christ of the past, but the living Christ of the present, is manifest through the liturgy of the Church.

"To accomplish so great a work, Christ is always present in His Church, especially in her liturgical celebrations. He is present in the sacrifice of the Mass, not only in the person of His minister, 'the same one now offering, through the ministry of priests, who formerly offered himself on the cross,' but especially under the Eucharistic species. By His power He is present in the sacraments, so that when a man baptizes it is really Christ Himself who baptizes. He is present in His word, since it is He Himself who speaks when the holy Scriptures are read in the church. He is present, finally, when the Church prays and sings, for He promised: 'Where two or three are gathered together for my sake, there am I in the midst of them' (Mt. 18:20)." (Art. 7.)

Therefore, from this it follows that every liturgical celebration, "because it is an action of Christ the priest and of His Body the Church," is a sacred action surpassing all others. Yet the sacred liturgy does not exhaust the entire activity of the Church, for before men can come to the liturgy they must first be called to faith and conversion. And in order that the liturgy may be able to produce its full effects, it is necessary that the faithful come to it with proper dispositions: "that their thoughts match their words, and that they cooperate with divine grace lest they receive it in vain." (Art. 11.) It is important, the decree says, that the faithful take part fully aware of what they are doing, actively engaged in the rite, and enriched personally by its effects.

Section II of Chapter I of the Constitution on the Sacred Liturgy is given over to the matter of proper liturgical instruction and active participation. This includes not only the faithful, but also priests, theological professors, those responsible for seminaries, and those engaged in mass communication.

Section III, on reform, instructs that to promote "active participation, the people should be encouraged to take part by means of acclamations, responses, psalmody, antiphons, and songs, as well as by actions, gestures, and bodily attitudes. And at the proper times all should observe a reverent silence." (Art. 30.)

In the revision of the liturgy these general norms are to be observed:

1. "The rites should be distinguished by a noble simplicity." (Art. 34.)

2. "In sacred celebrations there is to be more reading from holy Scripture." (Art. 35.)

3. The sermon is a part of the liturgical service and is to be fulfilled "with exactitude and fidelity." (Art. 35.)

4. "Bible services should be encouraged, especially on the vigils of the more solemn feasts, on some weekdays in Advent and Lent, and on Sundays and feast days." (Art. 35.)

5. The use of the mother tongue is to be extended, especially in regard "to the readings and directives and to some of the prayers and chants." (The extent of the use of the mother tongue is to be determined by the competent territorial ecclesiastical authority.) (Art. 36.)

In regard to the *simplicity of the rites* it is stressed that they should be "short, clear, and unencumbered by useless repetitions; they should be within the people's powers of comprehension." In regard to the *sermon* it is pointed out that its content should be drawn mainly from scriptural and liturgical sources and its character should be that "of a proclamation of God's wonderful works in the history of salvation, that is, the mystery of Christ, which is ever made present and active within us, especially in the celebration of the liturgy." It is emphasized that the liturgy in the *vernacular* may be of great advantage to the people.

Flexibility is also to be granted in relation to the culture and traditions of peoples—and no rigid uniformity is to be imposed.

> "Even in the liturgy, the Church has no wish to impose a rigid uniformity in matters which do not involve the faith or the good of the whole community. Rather she respects and fosters the spiritual adornments and gifts of the various races and peoples. Anything in their way of life that is not indissolubly bound up with superstition and error she studies with sympathy and, if possible, preserves intact. Sometimes in fact she admits such things into the liturgy itself, as long as they harmonize with its true and authentic spirit." (Ch. I, Art. 37.)

The Constitution then proceeds (Ch. I, Sections IV and V) to give specific directions to the bishops, and to liturgical commissions within each territorial ecclesiastical authority, to revise the liturgy according to the above principles, while keeping intact the dogmatic principles which were laid down by the Council of Trent. Moreover, the reform of the liturgy must be confined to the above-stated authority. Priests and the faithful are not to change the liturgy to suit their own purposes.

Listed for revision, in addition to the Mass, are (Ch. III): the rites for the baptism of adults and infants; for converts who have already been validly baptized; confirmation; penance; extreme unction (or better, the anointing of the sick); ordination; marriage; and sacramentals. Also: the consecration of virgins; religious profession and vows; the rite for burial of the dead; and the rite for the burial of infants.

In concelebration of the Mass—simultaneous celebration by more than one priest at the same altar—the unity of the priesthood is manifested; concelebration is to be re-emphasized (Ch. II, Art. 57) and a new rite is to be drawn up supporting it. While concelebration at the Lord's Table has been a common practice in the Eastern churches, and to a small extent in the West, it is now to become a regular practice, regulated by specific times and conditions stated in the Constitution. On several occasions at the Second Vatican Council concelebration was practiced along with the Pope. Concelebration is another indication that the bishops of the Church share a common ministry and responsibility.

Chapter IV is devoted to revisions of the Divine Office and it is noted that

"by tradition going back to early Christian times, the Divine Office is arranged so that the whole course of the day and night is made holy by the praises of God. Therefore, when this wonderful song of praise is worthily rendered by priests and others who are deputed for this purpose by Church ordinance, or by the faithful praying together with the priest in an approved form, then it is truly the voice of the bride addressing her bridegroom; it is the very prayer which Christ Himself, together with His body, addresses to the Father." (Art. 84.)

Chapter V deals with the liturgical year, and Chapter VI

with sacred music. In the latter the following points are made:

1. The musical tradition of the universal Church is a "treasure of immeasurable value." (Art. 112.)

2. Holy Scripture bestows praise upon sacred song.

3. Religious singing by the people is to be skillfully fostered "so that in devotions and sacred exercises, as also during liturgical services, the voices of the faithful may ring out according to the norms and requirements of the rubrics." (Art. 118.)

4. In certain parts of the world—as in mission lands—where people have their own musical traditions, a suitable place should be given to them in adapting worship to the native genius.

5. In the Latin Church the pipe organ is to be held in high esteem, but other instruments also may be admitted for use in divine worship (with the knowledge and consent of the competent territorial authority).

6. Composers are encouraged to feel that their vocation is to cultivate sacred music, not confining themselves to works which can be sung by large choirs, but "providing also for the needs of small choirs and for the active participation of the entire assembly of the faithful." (Art. 121.)

Chapter VII deals with sacred art and sacred furnishings, pointing out that the Church has always been the friend of the fine arts and that she has been particularly careful to see that sacred furnishings should worthily and beautifully serve the dignity of worship. The Church has never adopted any particular style of art as her very own, but has given free scope to it, provided that it adorns the sacred buildings and holy rites with due reverence and honor.

While the practice of placing sacred images in churches "so that they may be venerated by the faithful" is to be maintained, nevertheless their relative positions should reflect right order—"for otherwise they may create confusion among the Christian people and promote a faulty sense of devotion." (Art. 125.)

Along with the revision of liturgical books, there is to be a revision of the canons and ecclesiastical statutes which govern the provision of material things involved in sacred worship. These apply to the construction of sacred buildings, the shape and construction of altars, the eucharistic tabernacle, the baptistery, the proper ordering of sacred images, and the whole matter of vestments.

Pope Paul VI in his *motu proprio Sacram Liturgiam* (January 25, 1964) noted that it has always been the great concern of the papacy "to preserve, foster, and at need, reform" the sacred liturgy and gave instructions that certain parts of the reform should go into effect on the first Sunday of Lent, February 16, 1964, and that a special commission be created to bring to completion the matters prescribed in the Constitution on the Sacred Liturgy.

## II. THE PROTESTANT AND ORTHODOX POSITION

Protestant and Orthodox churches vary greatly in regard to the liturgy. In some denominations, following a radical Reformation approach, little emphasis is placed upon the liturgy; in fact, they oppose in particular the "sacerdotal" elements of the Mass and refrain in their public services and private devotions from anything pertaining to the sacerdotal. Yet during the past few years even many of these non-liturgical churches have been adding responses and chants to their services and have brought the altar into a central focus. Nevertheless, although there is a renewal of liturgical interest in these Protestant churches they are not at all of the Roman type. Therefore the judgment of these churches in regard to this Constitution on the Sacred Liturgy will be colored by Christian principles which do not fit exactly into the liturgical pattern.

On the other hand there are Protestant and Anglican churches which do have, while not on the same theological basis as the Roman Catholic Church, a strong liturgical structure. In particular the Lutheran churches and the Anglican churches follow this pattern. Their position in regard to this Constitution on the Sacred Liturgy will therefore be much more understanding and sympathetic, without accepting in full all of its theological premises.

Of still a different nature is the liturgical being of the Eastern Orthodox churches. Here the liturgical emphasis, and even the services, are quite similar to those of the Roman Catholic Church. This being the case, the Second Vatican Council (in the Decree on Ecumenism) made a special exception in regard to the Orthodox churches and under certain circumstances gave permission for an exchange, on an equal basis, of attendance at their liturgical services.

Dr. Douglas Horton, in writing of the differences between Roman Catholics and Protestants, declared that, although the differences are great, nevertheless there is at least a new understanding and appreciation of the spiritual significance behind the rites. "Our forms of worship are as remote from each other as the development of many centuries of symbolism is remote from everyday simplicity," he indicates in *Vatican Diary 1963* (United Church Press, p. 192). But, he goes on to say, "if after years of dialogue between the two churches we can come to understand the symbolism in each, we may well discover a community of understanding of which the difference in the forms as forms gives no hint."

Dr. Jaroslav Pelikan in *Obedient Rebel* (p. 91) points out the basic difference between Roman Catholicism and Protestantism as far as liturgy is concerned: in Roman Catholicism the liturgy is a legalistic matter; in Protestantism the liturgy is a matter of free choice. At the time of the Protestant Reformation people in the Church were required to conform to particular rites and ceremonies not prescribed by God.

> "So pervasive was the influence of that legalism that Luther was constrained to warn against the legalistic adoption of his own liturgical forms. At the very beginning of his *German Mass* he made it clear that the work was not to be used as liturgical legislation or as a snare for conscience. The circumstances and conditions of Christian congregations were so varied that it was not possible, even if it were permissible, to legislate any sort of liturgical uniformity. And at the end of the *German Mass* he reiterated the warning. When any liturgical form, including this one, had outlived its usefulness, it should be discarded. In and of itself it had no value."

As emphasized in the declaration of the Augsburg Confession, the unity of the Church was not to be found in any uniformity of rites created by men.

Dr. Vilmos Vajta, Director of the Lutheran Federation of Inter-Confessional Research, Geneva, Switzerland, in

*Dialogue on the Way* (Augsburg Publishing House), Chapter V, gives this appraisal of the Constitution on the Sacred Liturgy:

"We have seen which aspects of the liturgy are now being newly emphasized: the renewal of the use of Scripture in the liturgy, the proclamation of the mighty acts of God, the active participation of the faithful in worship on the basis of their baptism and, especially, the restoration of Communion in the eucharistic celebration. As every heir of the Reformation will easily see, these are precisely the elements which are fundamental for evangelical liturgical life. For this we must rejoice. Nevertheless, our analysis of the dogmatic presuppositions of the Constitution has shown that this kind of liturgical practice poses problems for Catholic dogmatics which have not yet been solved. This is evident in regard to the relation between the once-and-for-all sacrifice on the cross and the celebration of the present Lord in the eucharistic memorial. It is also evident in the failure to recognize clearly that the participation of the faithful in liturgical acts is a sharing through faith in God's saving acts. The gospel requires us to continue to raise these questions. But now they have become questions which are directed at Catholic dogmatics by liturgical practice itself as this has been legislated by this Constitution."

In the areas of agreement the changes brought by the Constitution on the Sacred Liturgy, and now in effect, are very marked and have a direct bearing upon every Protestant one way or another in every community.

What do the Protestant and Orthodox churches already have in common, as far as liturgy is concerned, with the Roman Catholic Church? They have in common these essential points:

1. The worship of Jesus Christ.

2. Two sacraments: baptism and the Lord's Supper. (The Orthodox have, as the Roman Catholics do, seven sacraments.)

3. Prayer—public and private.

4. Devotional literature, particularly that which was written prior to the Protestant Reformation.

5. Hymns and sacred music.

6. Ordination—priests and pastors.

7. The Bible, which is now used in identical versions.

8. Periods of devotion, such as Lent with Good Friday and Easter, and the Week of Prayer for Christian Unity.

9. Union services, especially of an ecumenical nature.

10. Many of the same basic aims in worship, as represented in the words of instruction by Christ.

Most every community has noticed the changes in attitude and practice which the Constitution on the Sacred Liturgy has made locally. These changes are reflected in Roman Catholic directives for ecumenical activities. For example, Roman Catholics are now permitted to:

—serve as witnesses at marriages which are celebrated in churches of other communions provided the marriage to be witnessed is a lawful one.

—have dialogues with non-Catholics about matters of liturgy.

—welcome Christians of other communions to Catholic liturgical celebrations.

—marry non-Catholics in the church itself, and the ceremony may take place during Mass. (The nuptial blessing, however, is not given in mixed marriages.)

—help to develop the ecumenical spirit and engage in ecumenical work.

—attend ecumenical services and certain prayer services (when specified by the bishop).

Catholic priests are now encouraged to:

—include prayers for unity within the liturgy.

—become acquainted with the clergy of Protestant and Orthodox churches and to work with them for the common good.

—join ministerial alliances and councils of churches.

—support dialogue groups.

—pray for the success of the World Council of Churches and the National Council of Churches, attend their social gatherings, and publicly commend their efforts.

—speak to groups of other communions in their parish halls or other suitable places outside the church and extend similar invitations to the clergy of these other communions.

—take part, in churches of other communions (outside the setting of the Lord's Supper or other official liturgy), when ecumenical services are held (for Christian unity, peace, in time of public need, mourning, or thanksgiving).

But neither priests nor members of the Roman Catholic Church are to participate in the Eucharistic celebrations or official worship services of Protestant churches. And while priests are permitted to officiate at the funeral services of members of other churches when these services take place in funeral parlors, or in the home, or at the graveside, they are not to officiate at funerals in the church of another communion. It is essential to note that burial in Catholic cemeteries may be permitted to members of other communions, especially to spouses and relatives of Catholics, and on such occasions clergymen of other churches may conduct graveside services.

Protestants ought to appreciate what Richard Cardinal Cushing of Boston says in his Foreword to the *Vatican II Edition of the Maryknoll Missal* published in 1966: "The Church has always shown special care for the liturgical service at which the faithful gather every Sunday. As the new Constitution says, 'The liturgy is the summit toward which the activity of the Church is directed; at the same time it is the fountain from which all her power flows.' " Protestants also ought to be challenged by the new *Missal* itself, for it represents all of the *aggiornamento* which the Constitution on the Sacred Liturgy so sincerely and dramatically presented to Catholics all over the world.

When Protestants wonder just how far they can go in common worship they should keep in mind that at the close of the Second Vatican Council Pope Paul VI joined in a service of prayer in which members of Protestant and Orthodox churches also participated. To be sure, there are certain limitations in common worship. Yet certain barriers have been broken down and a new spirit of cooperation has been established. Now it is possible, as never before, to join together in certain kinds of public worship; now it is possible to pray together; now it is possible to read the Bible together, even in the same version. It would be a tragic mistake if non-Catholics should not take full opportunity of this new situation.

Protestants, moreover, need to take lessons from both the Orthodox and the Roman Catholics (in the light of their new liturgy) in the ways and means of divine worship. Who can truly say that our Protestant worship services are as rich and meaningful as they should be? Who can truly maintain that our worship leads directly to God? Who can truly declare that Protestant worship involves the worshiper to any greater degree than does the new liturgy of the Roman Catholic Church? This Constitution on the Sacred Liturgy has not only created a much higher degree of Christian worship in the Catholic Church; it has challenged Protestants especially to take a fresh look at all their services of public worship, all of their books of prayers, every hymn book, to judge whether they are mere forms or idle words or whether they are means of bringing the true worshipers into the presence of the living and speaking God.

## III. QUESTIONS FOR DISCUSSION

1. Why is the Constitution on the Sacred Liturgy better known in the local Catholic community than any of the other documents of Vatican II?

2. What major changes did the Constitution make in the Roman Catholic liturgy?

3. What is the basic purpose of the changes in the liturgy?

4. To what degree are there "Protestant" elements in the new liturgy?

5. Why have non-Catholics welcomed the changes in the liturgy authorized by the Second Vatican Council?

6. To what extent can Catholics, Protestants, and the Orthodox now worship together?

7. What is meant by concelebration of the Mass?

8. When will Protestants, Anglicans, Orthodox, and Catholics be able to have a common celebration of the Lord's Supper?

9. Is a common celebration of the Eucharist necessary to the realization of Christian unity?

## IV. SUGGESTIONS FOR ECUMENICAL ACTION

1. Read carefully the Constitution on the Sacred Liturgy in *The Documents of Vatican II*.

2. Get a group together (Catholic, Protestant, and Orthodox if possible) to study the actual document under discussion (the Constitution on the Sacred Liturgy).

3. Attend an ecumenical prayer service.

4. (Protestant) Have a Roman Catholic priest explain the vestments and the actions of the Mass. (Catholic) Discuss with a Protestant pastor how the liturgy (worship service) of his church has changed during the past decade.

5. Attend a Mass which has modern musical accompaniments, such as a guitar or a jazz band.

6. Note how many "Protestant" hymns Catholics are now using, and vice versa.

> "By her relationship with Christ, the Church is a kind of sacrament or sign of intimate union with God, and of the unity of all mankind. She is also an instrument for the achievement of such union and unity. For this reason, following in the path laid out by its predecessors, this Council wishes to set forth more precisely to the faithful and to the entire world the nature and encompassing mission of the Church." (Dogmatic Constitution of the Church, Art. 1.)

# CHAPTER II

# The Nature
# of the Christian Church

## INTRODUCTION

From the point of view of the Roman Catholic Church this Dogmatic Constitution on the Church (*Lumen Gentium*) is considered by scholars to be the most important achievement of the Second Vatican Council. It was promulgated by Pope Paul VI on November 21, 1964. For the first time in history the inner nature and meaning of the Church was officially declared. Moreover, it was the long-awaited supplement of Vatican I because it developed the authoritative teaching of episcopal collegiality which will determine a basic structural reform in the entire Church. For the meaning of collegiality is this: that the bishops of the Catholic Church, in union with the Pope, constitute a body (or college) which is direct heir of the body of the Twelve, that is, the apostles with Peter as their head, which Christ made the very foundation of his Church.

This Constitution teaches:

1. That the Church itself is a mystery; that it is the Body of Christ; and that the true Church of Christ "subsists" in the Catholic Church.

2. That the Church is composed of the People of God; that the People of God, namely, all the baptized, participate in the priesthood of God and have a mandate through their baptism to profess their faith to the world.

3. That the doctrine of collegiality does not alter the authority of the Pope but rather supplements it.

4. That all within the Church are called to a life of holiness.

5. That the Church is a pilgrim Church and has a union with the Church in heaven.

6. That the Virgin Mary as the Mother of Christ should receive special veneration, but all such veneration must lead to Christ who alone is the Savior of men.

The ecumenical significance of this Constitution was noted by Pope Paul VI when he said in his closing speech at the third session:

> "We also hope that the same doctrine of the Church will be benevolently and favorably considered by the Christian brothers who are still separate from us. We wish that this doctrine, completed by the declarations contained in the schema on ecumenism, likewise approved by this Council, might have in their souls the power of a loving leaven for the revision of thoughts and attitudes which may draw them closer to our communion, and finally, God willing, may merge them in it."

# I. A SUMMARY OF THE DOGMATIC CONSTITUTION ON THE CHURCH

The Dogmatic Constitution on the Church is divided into eight chapters as follows: Chapter I—The Mystery of the Church; Chapter II—The People of God; Chapter III—Hierarchical Structure of the Church; Chapter IV—The Laity; Chapter V—Call of the Whole Church to Holiness; Chapter VI—Religious; Chapter VII—Eschatological Nature of the Pilgrim Church; Chapter VIII—The Blessed Virgin Mary.

Jesus, the Constitution declares, established the kingdom of God and, while the Catholic Church is not that kingdom, it "strains toward the consummation of the kingdom" and contributes to its realization. The Church is the Body of Christ and He is its head. Through Him truth and grace are communicated to all. "But the society furnished with hierarchical agencies and the Mystical Body of Christ are not to be considered as two realities, nor are the visible assembly and the spiritual community, nor the earthly Church and the Church enriched with heavenly things. Rather they form one interlocked reality which is comprised of a divine and a human element." This is the "unique Church of Christ" which Christians avow in the Creed as one, holy, catholic, and apostolic. This Church, constituted and organized in the world as a society, subsists in the Catholic Church, which is governed by the successor of Peter and by the bishops in union with that successor, although many elements of sanctification and of truth can be found outside of her visible structure. These elements, however, as gifts properly belonging to the Church of Christ, possess an inner dynamism toward Catholic unity." (Ch. I, Art. 8.)

As Gregory Baum, O.S.A., says in a commentary on this passage (*Study-Club Edition: The Dogmatic Constitution on the Church*, Deus Books, Paulist Press), "According to Catholic faith, only the Catholic Church perfectly embodies the Church of Christ on earth, but, because of the transcendence of Christ's Church, this does not preclude the possibility that there may be partial realizations of this Church among men." Here, for the first time, the Catholic Church recognizes non-Catholic congregations as Churches.

In Chapter II the Constitution emphasizes, and gives a special priority (even before the chapter on the hierarchy) to the "People of God." It thus places grace before institutionalism. And although laity and clergy differ in functions and callings they constitute the same "one priesthood of Christ." "Though they differ from one another in essence and not only in degree, the common priesthood of the faithful and the ministerial or hierarchical priesthood are nonetheless interrelated. Each of them in its own special way is a participation in the one priesthood of Christ." (Art. 10.)

All the faithful (the word "members" is not used) of

the Church are called to worship and holiness; to a share in the prophetic office of Christ; to a living witness before men; and to missionary work. In the section on the status of the laity (which is considered in Chapter IV of the Constitution), service in the world is spelled out in detail.

Chapter III deals with the hierarchical structure of the Church and the episcopate in particular. It closely follows Vatican I in declaring that Christ established the Church and placed Peter over the other apostles "and instituted in him a permanent and visible source and foundation of unity of faith and fellowship." It also declared the sacred primacy of the Roman Pontiff "and of his infallible teaching authority."

Then it proceeds, on the basis of what was begun at Vatican I, to proclaim what is known as the collegiality of the bishops. "Continuing in the same task of clarification begun by Vatican I, this Council has decided to declare and proclaim before all men its teaching concerning bishops, the successors of the apostles, who together with the successor of Peter, the Vicar of Christ and the visible Head of the whole Church, govern the house of the living God." (Art. 18.)

Attention is called in this chapter to bishops as direct successors of the apostles, indicating that "the chief place belongs to the office of those who, appointed to the episcopate in a sequence running back to the beginning, are the ones who pass on the apostolic seed." These bishops preside "in place of God over the flock." Moreover, through episcopal consecration the bishops have received a special outpouring of the Holy Spirit giving them spiritual gifts. "Therefore, this sacred Synod teaches that by divine institution bishops have succeeded to the place of the apostles as shepherds of the Church, and that he who hears them, hears Christ, while he who rejects them, rejects Christ and Him who sent Christ (cf. Lk. 10:16)." (Art. 20.)

These bishops of the Church, along with the Pope, constitute one apostolic college, so that they are joined together. But it is clearly understood that the Roman Pontiff, as the successor of Peter, is supreme and that his power of primacy over all, both pastors and the faithful, remains whole and intact, and he is always free to exercise this power alone.

The principle of collegiality is based upon the sharing

of divine authority between the bishops and the Pope—but never without the Pope. Moreover this power of joint authority can be exercised "only with the consent of the Roman Pontiff." The supreme power of this body is exercised in a solemn way in an ecumenical council with the Pope as its head.

The matter of infallibility looms large at the very heart of this chapter on the hierarchical structure of the Church. Although individual bishops do not enjoy the prerogative of infallibility, as does the Pope, nevertheless they can "proclaim Christ's doctrine infallibly . . . even when they are dispersed around the world, provided that while maintaining the bond of unity among themselves and with Peter's successor, and while teaching authentically on a matter of faith or morals, they concur in a single viewpoint as the one which must be held conclusively." (Art. 25.) This is especially true when they meet and act in relation to an ecumenical council.

Infallibility of the Pope, in view of his office, is indicated as follows:

"This infallibility with which the divine Redeemer willed His Church to be endowed in defining a doctrine of faith and morals extends as far as extends the deposit of divine revelation, which must be religiously guarded and faithfully expounded. This is the infallibility which the Roman Pontiff, the head of the college of bishops, enjoys in virtue of his office, when, as the supreme shepherd and teacher of all the faithful, who confirms his brethren in their faith (cf. Lk. 22:32), he proclaims by a definitive act some doctrine of faith or morals. Therefore his definitions, of themselves, and not from the consent of the Church, are justly styled irreformable, for they are pronounced with the assistance of the Holy Spirit, an assistance promised to him in blessed Peter. Therefore they need no approval of others, nor do they allow an appeal to any other judgment. For then the Roman Pontiff is not pronouncing judgment as a private person. Rather, as the supreme teacher of the universal Church, as one in whom the charism of the infallibility of the Church herself is individually present, he is expounding or defending a doctrine of Catholic faith." (Art. 25.)

Thus the doctrine of papal infallibility which was defined by Vatican Council I was confirmed *in toto* and what Vatican I did not complete, that is, extending infallibility to the bishops through collegiality, Vatican II proceeded to establish.

It is important to note that the bishops have entrusted to them the pastoral office and the daily care of their sheep, and they are not to be regarded as vicars of the Roman Pontiff, "for they exercise an authority that is proper to them, and are quite correctly called 'prelates,' heads of the people whom they govern." (Art. 27.) Priests, by the power of the sacrament of orders, share with and under the direction of the bishops. Priests announce the divine Word to all, serve in the Eucharistic liturgy "acting in the person of Christ" and acting as pastors in a ministry of alleviation and reconciliation. (Art. 28.)

Deacons are at a lower level of the hierarchy upon whom hands are imposed " 'not unto the priesthood, but unto a ministry of service.' " (Art. 29.) Stress was placed upon giving the diaconate its proper place in the hierarchy, because of the needs of this kind of service in various parts of the world. It is significant to note that "with the consent of the Roman Pontiff, this diaconate will be able to be conferred upon men of more mature age, even upon those living in the married state." It is also conferred upon suitable young men for whom the law of celibacy remains intact.

Vatican Council II gave a higher status to the laity as indicated in Chapter IV of the Dogmatic Constitution on the Church. The laity of the Church has this connotation: "The term laity is here understood to mean all the faithful except those in holy orders and those in a religious state sanctioned by the Church. These faithful are by baptism made one body with Christ and are established among the People of God. They are in their own way made sharers in the priestly, prophetic, and kingly functions of Christ. They carry out their own part in the mission of the whole Christian people with respect to the Church and the world." (Art. 31.)

It is because of their secular nature that the laity have a special calling in the modern world. Their vocation is in the world. This is why the laity, by their special placement, "seek the kingdom of God by engaging in temporal affairs and by ordering them according to the plan of God."

Even the lowest member of the laity has the right to be heard in the Church. (It is said that Vatican I was the council of the papacy, and Vatican II was the council of the laity.) Therefore, the priest or pastor must always keep the laity in mind and do everything possible to help them fulfill their ministry in the home, community, and world.

Although having a special ministry in the world, nevertheless the laity have no role in the government of the Church and are under the direction of the clergy in most respects.

Chapter V deals with the call of the whole Church to holiness, pointing out that "all the faithful of Christ of whatever rank and status are called to the fullness of the Christian life and to the perfection of charity." (Art. 40.) Here there are no exceptions; the Pope, the bishops, all the clergy, and all laymen are called to live a life of devotion and holiness.

Chapter VI, on the religious, indicates that the religious state of life is not an intermediate state between the clerical and lay states, but rather those "called by God from both these states of life so that they may enjoy this particular gift in the life of the Church." These faithful of Christ represent persons who are totally dedicated to God, belonging to various orders of the Church.

Chapter VII is on the eschatological nature of the pilgrim Church and her union with the heavenly Church. Here in the visible Church we learn the meaning of our terrestrial life through our faith, while at the same time "we perform, with hope of good things to come, the task committed to us in this world by the Father, and work out our salvation (cf. Phil. 2:12)." (Art. 48.) Moreover, there is a connection between those on earth and those who have proceeded on ahead, and "they do not cease to intercede with the Father for us." "The Church has always believed that the apostles, and Christ's martyrs who had given the supreme witness of faith and charity by the shedding of their blood, are quite closely joined with us in Christ. She has always venerated them with special devotion, together with the Blessed Virgin Mary and the holy angels. The Church too has devoutly implored the aid of their intercession." (Art. 50.)

This leads directly to Chapter VIII on the role of the Blessed Virgin Mary, Mother of God, in the Mystery of Christ and the Church. "In this Church, adhering to Christ the Head and having communion with all His saints, the faithful must also venerate the memory 'above all of the glorious and perpetual Virgin Mary, Mother of our God and Lord Jesus Christ.' " (Art. 52.)

After making references to Mary's earthly relationship to Christ, from birth to the resurrection, and referring to her birth without sin and her assumption into heaven, it says: "Finally, preserved free from all guilt of original sin, the Immaculate Virgin was taken up body and soul into heavenly glory upon the completion of her earthly sojourn. She was exalted by the Lord as Queen of all, in order that she might be the more thoroughly conformed to her Son, the Lord of lords (cf. Apoc. 19:16) and the conqueror of sin and death." (Art. 59.)

Although there is only one mediator of God and men, that is, Christ, and the special blessings and powers of Mary do not obscure or diminish this unique mediation of Christ, nevertheless she does have a "salvific influence" which fosters, rather than impedes, the immediate union of the faithful with Christ. The Constitution declares that "the Church does not hesitate to profess this subordinate role of Mary." (Art. 62.) It goes on to point out that "when she is preached and venerated, she summons the faithful to her Son and His sacrifice and to the love for the Father." (Art. 65.) And while it supports the special cult of Mary in the Church it warns against abuses. It plainly states that true devotion to Mary "consists neither in fruitless and passing emotion, nor in a certain vain credulity. Rather, it proceeds from true faith, by which we are led to know the excellence of the Mother of God, and are moved to a filial love toward our mother and to the imitation of her virtues." (Art. 67.)

The last paragraph of the Constitution declares that the Council has joy and comfort in the fact that even among the separated brethren, and especially the Orthodox, there are many who give honor to Mary as the Mother of God. It then closes with these words:

"Let the entire body of the faithful pour forth persevering prayer to the Mother of God and Mother of men. Let them implore that she who aided the beginnings of the Church by her prayers may now, exalted as she is in heaven above all the saints and angels, intercede with her Son in the fellowship of all the saints. May she do so until all the peoples of the human family, whether they are honored with the name of Christian or whether they still do not know their Savior, are happily gathered together in peace and harmony into one People of God, for the glory of the Most Holy and Undivided Trinity."

# II. NON-CATHOLICS AND THE CHURCH

Protestants, on the whole, look upon the Reformation of the sixteenth century as a period of reform and renewal of the Church and not as a break with the true Church of Christ. They do not consider, because Martin Luther was excommunicated by the Pope, that their churches or denominations are outside the scope of the full benefits of grace or the full power of the Holy Spirit. In fact, Protestants believe that, as far as the practice of the Church of the New Testament is concerned, they actually have an advantage over the Roman Catholic Church.

On the other hand, the Roman Catholic Church, even taking into consideration the new attitudes of the Second Vatican Council, still claims to be the "only true Church" (see, for example, the Introduction of the Declaration on Religious Freedom) and that the other non-Catholic churches belong to the true Church only in such measure as they partake of the spirit, principles, and faith of the Roman Catholic Church.

To complicate the situation the Eastern Orthodox Church also claims to be the "only true Church." And so do several sects. Most every denomination, large or small, proclaims distinctive practices or beliefs which, from their point of view, raise them above the status of separate sects and justify their being the true Church or at least a real part of the true Church.

Dr. George A. Lindbeck, of Yale Divinity School, in presenting a paper on "The Theological Issues of Vatican II" at the International Conference on the Main Theological Issues of Vatican II at the University of Notre Dame in 1966, pointed out that although the Dogmatic Constitution on the Church, from the Protestant point of view, is a highly ambiguous document, "it does nevertheless represent a watershed in the history of the Roman Catholic Church that is likely to have consequences beyond the present possibility of our imagining." Being a compromise, Dr. Lindbeck said, it can be understood in radically different ways by honest and competent scholars. Whereas he was pleased with its emphasis on the Church as the People of God, he wished that this might have received greater prominence. Moreover, he notes that the point where the uncertainties of the non-Catholic becomes greatest is in reference to the treatment of the episcopacy and of collegiality. This is due not only to a rather irresponsible use of Scripture, but to the fact that it is impossible, from the text itself, to determine whether collegiality includes the People of God in a radical structural transformation or merely completes Vatican I in giving the bishops divine authority in the government of the Church along with the Pope. In view of these ambiguities Dr. Lindbeck fears that the Dogmatic Constitution on the Church may not develop on its "progressive" side, but will revert, as in the past, to a strict dogmatic and institutional position. A Protestant, he maintains, cannot regard such a prospect with any enthusiasm.

> "If this Constitution operates as a conclusion, not a transition, if Catholic thinking and attitudes are stamped into a kind of simulacrum of its compromises and ambiguities, then the last state, while no doubt better than the first, will not be much better. Catholics will then continue to be trained to think and feel about a wide range of topics, but especially about ecclesiastical authority in general and the bishops and Pope in particular, in a way that not only Protestants and Orthodox, but even some of the most impressive contemporary Roman Catholic voices, would describe as unbiblical and sub-Christian."

If, on the other hand, the Roman Catholic Church moves forward with emphasis on an eschatological view of the world and to the theme of the pilgrim People of God, then the whole Church will in its transformation proceed finally into the Kingdom of God where it will find other Christians and the ultimate Christian unity.

At the Fourth World Conference on Faith and Order, held by the World Council of Churches in Montreal in 1963, the subject of the Church and the Churches was handled as follows:

> "In our discussion of the relation of the churches to the church we have found it helpful to think not in terms of the churches as parts of the one church, but rather of the church as the Body of Christ, including the saints of all ages and the Christians of all places, which is both present in, and one with, the local congregation gathered for the hearing of the Word and the celebration of the Lord's Supper according to Christ's ordinance. 'Wherever Jesus Christ is, there is the Catholic Church.' "

Here, of course, the word *Catholic* applies to the entire Church (Protestant, Orthodox, Anglican, and Roman Catholic) and not just to the Roman branch of it. Moreover, it does not indicate so much participation in some ecclesiastical organization as an identification with Christ. In this sense each congregation is a manifestation of the whole Church.

Some Protestants believe that their ecclesiastical institutions fully manifest the one true Church, while others would want to add that no community can fully manifest the one true Church; nevertheless all would recognize that in these Christian communities Christ is present and that His lordship is acknowledged and that their members in some degree therefore belong to the one true Church.

The major differences in relation to the Church, between Protestants and Roman Catholics, are at these three points: (1) in regard to the Church itself as a saving institution; (2) in relation to the Church as being in any sense "infallible"; and (3) pertaining to the Church being founded upon Peter. All Protestant and Orthodox churches, although they may differ slightly as to the degree of their belief, do not regard the Church *per se* as a saving institution, do not believe it to be "infallible," and do not believe that it was founded upon Peter.

In order to discover some of the real differences between the Roman Catholic Church and the Orthodox and Protestant churches let us note the following points which will have to be considered in any serious ecumenical dialogue:

**ORTHODOX DIFFERENCES.** The Orthodox churches have many points of agreement with the Roman Catholic Church (such as the seven sacraments, certain creedal statements, liturgies, and apostolic tradition), but they also disagree with it at the following points:

1. They do not accept the dogma of the immaculate conception of the Virgin Mary; the Orthodox believe that although the Virgin Mary was not exempt from original sin, from which she was cleansed at the time of the Annunciation, by the grace of God she did not commit any actual sin.

2. They do not accept the dogma that the Church was founded upon Peter. Instead they believe that Christ clearly said that His Church is built upon the truth which Peter declared, namely, that Jesus Christ is the Son of the living God. The Orthodox therefore indicate that only through "considerable distortion" of the Scripture text (Mt. 16:13-18) can one draw the conclusion that Christ founded His Church upon "Peter."

3. They do not accept the primacy of jurisdiction of the Pope, maintaining that the Scriptures do not declare that Peter had authority over the other apostles. In fact, they question whether Peter had any actual and personal relationship to the Church of Rome. They point out that he went to Rome where he suffered martyrdom only after a long service to the Church in Antioch.

**PROTESTANT DIFFERENCES.** Like the Orthodox churches, the Protestant churches (1) do not accept the primacy of the Pope and (2) do not believe that the Church was founded upon Peter, but rather upon Christ. Unlike both the Roman Catholic Church and the Orthodox churches Protestants do not accept seven sacraments, but only two (baptism and the Lord's Supper); moreover, Protestantism does not accept either of the other two Christian faiths as being the one true Church. Although the Dogmatic Constitution on the Church does much to raise the Church above mere institutionalism and opens up the whole area of the Church as mystery, most Protestants, even while considering the new doctrine of collegiality as somewhat of an advancement in ecclesiastical democracy, nevertheless do not accept the position of the Vatican II document that the bishops, as well as the Pope, received their divine commission directly in line of succession from the apostles. Many of them may believe in "apostolic succession" on a practical or administrative pastoral basis, but relatively few believe that the authority and direction of the Church is in the absolute possession of a divinely established hierarchy separated from the laity.

The Church, according to the section report of the Fourth World Conference on Faith and Order, "is the 'new creation' precisely as the body of the crucified-risen Lord. Even as Christ's glory is revealed in His self-humiliation, so in Christ the Church is called and enabled to manifest the 'new creation' in obedient discipleship and faithful servanthood in the world."

## III. QUESTIONS FOR DISCUSSION

1. What are the basic differences between Roman Catholic and non-Catholic churches?·

2. Why cannot Orthodox and Protestant churches accept the dogma that the Church is founded upon Peter?

3. Where does the "authority" rest in Catholic, Orthodox, and Protestant churches?

4. At what points are all Christian faiths in total agreement in relation to the nature of the Church?

5. Why is it not yet possible for Catholics, Orthodox, and Protestants to hold united Communion services?

6. What are the major blocks to Church union?

7. What great steps toward Christian unity have been made during the past decade?

8. What bearing does the Consultation on Church Union [1] have in regard to Protestant-Catholic relations?

## IV. SUGGESTIONS FOR ECUMENICAL ACTION

1. Read the text of the Dogmatic Constitution on the Church in *The Documents of Vatican II*.

[1] The Consultation on Church Union is a group of nine denominations in the U.S.A. now considering possible steps toward forming a new united church. This Consultation was created as a result of a sermon preached by the Rev. Dr. Eugene Carson Blake just prior to a meeting of the National Council of Churches in San Francisco (December, 1960). (See *Where We Are in Church Union*, paperback, 75c, Association Press.)

2. Protestants, attend a Roman Catholic Church and note the major points of likeness and difference with your own church.

3. Form an interfaith study group to study the documents of Vatican II, beginning with the Dogmatic Constitution on the Church.

4. Discover how the Eastern Orthodox Church differs from both the Roman Catholic Church and Protestant churches.

5. The Dogmatic Constitution on the Church is called in Latin *Lumen Gentium*. Find out what this term means.

"But since the word of God should be available at all times, the Church with maternal concern sees to it that suitable and correct translations are made into different languages, especially from the original texts of the sacred books. And if, given the opportunity and the approval of Church authority, these translations are produced in cooperation with the separated brethren as well, all Christians will be able to use them." (Dogmatic Constitution on Divine Revelation, Art. 22.)

## CHAPTER III

# The Holy Bible and Tradition

## INTRODUCTION

During the first session of the Second Vatican Council, the Theological Commission presented a schema whose intent and effect would have been practically to equate tradition with Scripture as a second source of Revelation. This would not have been the crystallization of an ancient doctrine, but was actually contrary to Trent and First Vatican Councils (see Dr. Frederick C. Grant's "Response," in *The Documents of Vatican II*).

The Commission had twice before refused to confer with the Secretariat for the Promotion of Christian Unity, Bishop de Smedt revealed. When the schema came to a preliminary vote, it was opposed by about seven-elevenths of the bishops, whereas two-thirds were required for rejection. In the most dramatic and probably the most fateful action of that session, Pope John XXIII treated the vote as a rejection and created a mixed commission including a dozen bishops from the Secretariat, with Cardinal Bea and Cardinal Ottaviani as co-chairmen. The announcement was made on November 24, 1962.

The role of Cardinal Bea is particularly worthy of note. For years he was head of the Pontifical Biblical Institute, which moved in the direction of genuine scholarship, something that the professors at the Lateran University, also in Rome, found highly distasteful and dangerous. He was also the confessor of Pius XII, whose encyclical, *Divino Afflante Spiritu* (1943) gave substantial encouragement to freer study of the Bible. (During World War II when a Y.M.C.A. representative working with Italian prisoners of war in Africa told Pope Pius of a shortage of Roman Catholic Bibles, the Pope said, "The Bible must be read, even without the useful notes: use a Protestant version.")

A possible reason for the insistence by some Roman Catholics on the practical autonomy of the tradition (admitted at least privately during Vatican II) is the lack of evidence in the New Testament for some of the Mariological doctrines. In question also are the meaning of the supremacy of Peter among the apostles, the juridical interpretation of the Keys,[1] and the succession of the Bishop of Rome to St. Peter's authority. While it cannot be said that the new Constitution resolves completely the relationship of tradition to Scripture, it frees theologians for further study and interpretation, with scholarly methods and in cooperation with Protestant and Eastern Orthodox theologians.

The changed tone and spirit of the new Constitution was foreshadowed by Pope Paul's approval in April, and the publication in June, 1964, by the Pontifical Biblical Commission, of "An Instruction Concerning the Historical Truth of the Gospels." This included both permission and caution for the use of form criticism,[2] distinguished inerrancy from historicity, outlined the three stages in the

[1] The interpretation of "the Keys" (Mt. 16:19) by the Roman Catholic Church is as follows: that the Pope, as the successor of St. Peter, has the full powers of the Keys, i.e., the spiritual jurisdiction of the Church. Bishops, and also priests, participate in the powers in lesser degrees. In virtue of this "power," sin can be forgiven, indulgences granted, and penalties may be inflicted on members of the Church.

[2] "Form criticism" (*Formgeschichte*) is the historical investigation of the New Testament beyond the stage of the earliest written gospel to penetrate the "silent period when the stories and sayings of Jesus were imprinted on the parchment of the human memory."

development of the Christian tradition, and warned against overemphasis on the adjective "creative" as applied to the Christian community's role in the third stage, saying that it was rather "formative." It also affirmed that variation in the order of events chronicled by the gospel writers does not affect their authentic portrayal of gospel truth.

It was not until September 30, 1964, twenty-two months after Pope John's intervention, that the mixed Commission submitted to the Council a new draft for the Constitution on Divine Revelation. Even then there was a minority *relator* (spokesman) and another for the majority. The latter was Archbishop Florit (now a cardinal). In a special, encyclopedic issue of *Osservatore della Domenica* (undated) early in 1966, giving the substance of the text and a brief history of each of the sixteen documents of Vatican II, the commentator on this Constitution is Cardinal Florit. (Quotations from his commentary are indicated by *O.d.D.*)

The document, *Dei Verbum,* was promulgated by Pope Paul VI on November 18, 1965.


# I. THE DOGMATIC CONSTITUTION ON DIVINE REVELATION

The Constitution, quoting 1 Jn. 1:2-3, and "following in the footsteps of the Councils of Trent and of First Vatican," consists of six chapters: I: Revelation Itself; II: The Transmission of Divine Revelation; III: The Divine Inspiration and the Interpretation of Sacred Scripture; IV: The Old Testament; V: The New Testament; VI: Sacred Scripture in the Life of the Church. This practically adds up to the Roman Catholic doctrine of the Bible.

**THE REVELATION.** The Bible is treated as a means, a channel of the revelation. The revelation is God's manifestation of Himself primarily, and of His will and intentions, and becomes clear to us in Christ, "who is the Mediator and at the same time the fullness of all revelation" (Art. 2), the Word made Flesh. Cardinal Florit comments *(O.d.D.):* "Consequently, Christianity is more than a doctrine, it is a divine fact: the very Incarnation of God."

The historical steps in revelation are briefly described

up to the Christian dispensation, which, it is stated, "as the new and definitive covenant, will never pass away." (Art. 4.) The next paragraph refers, however, to the help of the Holy Spirit "to bring about an ever deeper understanding of revelation." (Art. 5.)

**THE TRANSMISSION.** Cardinal Florit says that the Council thought it wise to exclude the phrase "sources of revelation," which had "entered into use in recent epoch," as "inappropriate and susceptible of interpretations not always exact." *(O.d.D.)*

Scripture includes the revelation received by the apostles. We must remember that it was handed along orally before it was reduced to writing. In turn, it has to be handed along to congregations and individuals—this is, literally, tradition: at any moment in its static and substantive sense, a body of accepted truth; in its dynamic sense, the process by which revelation is assimilated into Christian belief—a process just as necessary for Protestants as for Catholics, though the process is not actually or necessarily the same in all times and places. Tradition does not add to revelation, but only to its more complete perception and understanding. As the Constitution has it (Ch. II, Art. 8): "For, as the centuries succeed one another, the Church constantly moves forward toward the fullness of divine truth until the words of God reach their complete fulfillment in her."

The chapter on transmission is the relatively novel section of the Constitution, says Cardinal Florit, in that it treats of tradition (which in one sense includes Scripture) in relation to the Bible, to the teaching of the Church, and to its life.

Scripture of the Old and New Testaments, and tradition, taken together, "are like a mirror in which the pilgrim Church on earth looks at God, from whom she has received everything, until she is brought finally to see Him as He is, face to face (cf. 1 Jn. 3:2)." (Ch. II, Art. 7.)

The chapter as a whole would seem to be clear and vigorous in rejecting the thesis (or hypothesis) of *sola scriptura*. The Cardinal tells us however that it was only a short time before the general vote on the Constitution that this sentence was inserted (Ch. II, Art. 9): "Consequently, it is not from sacred Scripture alone that the Church draws her certainty about everything which has been revealed." A footnote in *The Documents of Vatican*

*II* (p. 117) indicates that Pope Paul called for this addition, and adds: "It does not exclude the opinion that all revelation is in some way, though perhaps obscurely, contained in Scripture." Cardinal Florit comments that the addition can be understood in the light of the whole Constitution, from which he says it is clear "that neither is the tradition presented as a quantitative supplement to Scripture, nor is Scripture presented as a codification of the entire Revelation." He adds that "to the apostles is to be attributed the formation of the tradition, and to the bishops instead its conservation, exposition, and diffusion." *(O.d.D.)*

**INSPIRATION AND INTERPRETATION OF SCRIPTURE.** "Therefore, since everything asserted by the inspired authors or sacred writers must be held to be asserted by the Holy Spirit, it follows that the books of Scripture must be acknowledged as teaching firmly, faithfully, and without error that truth which God wanted put into the sacred writings for the sake of our salvation. Therefore 'all Scripture is inspired by God and useful for teaching, for reproving, for correcting, for instruction in justice; that the man of God may be perfect, equipped for every good work' (2 Tim. 3:16-17, Greek text)." (Ch. III, Art. 11.)

"However, since God speaks in sacred Scripture through men in human fashion, the interpreter of sacred Scripture, in order to see clearly what God wanted to communicate to us, should carefully investigate what meaning the sacred writers really intended, and what God wanted to manifest by means of their words." (Art. 12.)

The third chapter continues by taking account of the need and legitimate use of form criticism, and emphasizes that the whole of Scripture must be considered, under the guidance of the same Holy Spirit who inspired it, in interpreting its parts. The chapter allows considerable freedom to theologians in their exegesis, which is to help in maturing the Church's judgment, but "is subject finally" to that judgment.

Inerrancy is thus not a verbal phenomenon, nor is it historical in the ordinary sense. What is indicated is inerrancy for salvific faith; Father Barnabas Ahern, who was a helpful member of the American bishops' press panel, has suggested "soteriological inerrancy."

**THE OLD AND NEW TESTAMENTS.** Both are treated from the point of view of salvation history; each is necessary to the other. "God, the inspirer and author of both testaments, wisely arranged that the New Testament be hidden in the Old and the Old be made manifest in the New." (Ch. IV, Art. 16.)

"The Gospels have a special pre-eminence, and rightly so, for they are the principal witness of the life and teaching of the incarnate Word, our Savior." (Ch. V, Art. 18.) They are of apostolic origin. They "faithfully hand on what Jesus Christ, while living among men, really did and taught for their eternal salvation . . ." (Ch. V, Art. 19.) The authors wrote sometimes selecting from their oral or written sources, sometimes synthesizing, again "explicating" (a word taken from the 1964 "Instruction" of the Pontifical Biblical Commission—see above), "but always in such fashion that they told us the honest truth about Jesus." (Art. 19.)

**SACRED SCRIPTURE IN THE LIFE OF THE CHURCH.** "For in the sacred books, the Father who is in heaven meets His children with great love and speaks with them; and the force and power in the word of God is so great that it remains the support and energy of the Church, the strength of faith for her sons, the food of the soul, the pure and perennial source of spiritual life." (Ch. VI, Art. 21.)

And now comes real *aggiornamento:* "Easy access to sacred Scripture should be provided for all the Christian faithful." (Art. 22.) It was not always thus. In the same article there follows the passage permitting common translations for ecumenical use, quoted at the beginning of this chapter.

Study of the Fathers of both East and West, and of different liturgies, is recommended. ". . . as many ministers of the divine word as possible will [then] be able effectively to provide the nourishment of the Scriptures for the People of God . . ." Biblical scholars are encouraged "to continue energetically with the work they have so well begun." (Art. 23.)

"Sacred theology rests on the written word of God, together with sacred tradition, as its primary and perpetual foundation . . . the sacred Scriptures contain the word of God and, since they are inspired, really are the word of God. . . ." (Art. 24.) "Therefore, all the clergy must hold fast to the sacred Scriptures through diligent sacred reading and careful study. . . ." So, too, must all the faithful, " 'For ignorance of the Scriptures is ignorance of Christ' " (quotation from St. Jerome). Let them "remember that prayer should accompany the reading of sacred Scripture, so that God and man may talk together. . . ." The bishops are responsible for "instruction in the right use of the divine books . . . with necessary and fully adequate explanations . . . editions . . . with suitable comments . . . also for the use of non-Christians. . . ." (Art. 25.)

In the final article (26), the nourishment of the sacred books is compared with that of the Eucharist: persistence is vital.

## II. CLOSING THE GAP

The adoption of the draft submitted during the first session of Vatican II on the sources of revelation would have added hurtfully to the Roman Catholic tradition by confirming the misunderstandings that were growing up, and would have widened the gap between Roman Catholics and non-Romans. Instead, the gap is being closed from both sides. Cardinal Florit referred to Protestant-Orthodox discussions at Montreal, 1963, as a step in understanding tradition. Dr. Albert Outler—who was active at Montreal —has recently observed that Protestants may have reached the end of *sola scriptura* as their authority; the Church has become the matrix of truth as well as of redemption.

One important approach to the matter is to recognize *tradition* as a process; traditions that vary with times and confessions; and *the tradition,* as the truth, the revelation, the central core of Christian faith. One has often observed Protestants attacking Roman Catholic tradition as though tradition were of little account, without realizing that they were simply opposing to it a Protestant, even a sectarian, tradition. Now, in fact, the Council, in this Constitution, has refused to confirm what Protestants have been rightly criticizing. While the Council has, according to Bishop

Wright (*Dialogue #33*, p. 39),[3] bypassed the old polemic about the sources of revelation, "it puts the claims made on behalf of Scripture and those made in behalf of tradition in proper subordination to Christ Himself as the supreme way in which the Father speaks to us in the new dispensation."

Not all Protestants will agree with Dr. Outler on the nature and importance of tradition; not all Roman Catholics will be happy over the failure to exalt tradition still further. But barriers have been somewhat lowered, and Catholic theologians can now feel free and authorized to continue the discussion ecumenically—a freedom that most Protestants have long enjoyed, but a freedom that calls for more discipline than some of them have sometimes employed!

The disciplines prescribed in the 1964 "Instruction" of the Pontifical Biblical Commission, and in the Constitution itself, are those generally observed by serious biblicists and theologians. But both Protestant and Catholic believers are still largely addicted to proof texts,[4] and to interpretations that are undermined when the testimony of Scripture as a whole is heeded.

Dr. Paul Minear feels that Vatican II encouraged "an accent on the words rather than the life-giving fellowship with God, on the 'deposit' of Jesus' teaching rather than the living presence of the Crucified Lord." Such a tendency is difficult to avoid in an authoritarian institution: one can prescribe and defend a formula better than one can promote spirituality. Yet Vatican II in almost every document moved in the direction of appreciation of the Bible, the centrality of Jesus Christ, the indispensable role of the Holy Spirit, and the wholeness of the Christian experience and doctrine—not least in the Dogmatic Constitution on Divine Revelation.

While the way for dialogue is open as it had not been since 1054 and the Great Schism—certainly not since the Reformation—dialogue itself is hampered, and gravely, as

[3] The *Dialogue* referred to here is one of a series of booklets containing the Religious News Service reports of all four sessions of the Second Vatican Council. They are published by the National Conference of Christians and Jews.

[4] "Proof texts" refers to verses of Scripture taken out of context to prove a particular point. The actual meaning of such a verse removed from its context is usually different from that of its original intent. Therefore, modern scholarship disapproves of using Scripture in such a manner.

long as it is begun with presuppositions on either side which if known would be summarily rejected by the other, and if suspected weaken the process before it begins. If one suspects that the other is insincere, condescending, arrogant, more paternal than fraternal—perhaps only a dialogue begun in spite of doubts and fears can remove the suspicions. This has happened—in the Council itself, among Protestants, between the Confessions—and is happening more and more.

It must happen widely and earnestly with regard to Revelation, Scripture, Tradition, the Teaching. The Constitution carefully reserves the final authority of the Church at several points. Formally, that means the Roman Catholic Church. But the partly invisible Church, and the divided Church, are implicit both in Council documents, and, increasingly, in the thought and speech of Roman Catholics, Protestants, and Eastern Orthodox. It is of course the Church in its unity that can be or become the matrix of truth and redemption.

# III. QUESTIONS FOR DISCUSSION

1. Why do laymen need to concern themselves with ecumenical questions? Why not leave them to the clergy?

2. What is the real meaning of "the priesthood of all believers"?

3. What would agreement as to what the tradition is, and how to interpret it, do for the approach toward Christian unity?

4. Why is this decree on Scripture and tradition considered of special benefit to the ecumenical movement?

5. What progress is being made toward a common Bible?

6. Why should the Bible play a more important role in all Christian relationship?

7. How do Jews interpret the New Testament?

8. Is the Holy Spirit still revealing new truth?

# IV. SUGGESTIONS FOR ECUMENICAL ACTION

1. Read the comments of the Rev. R. A. F. Mackenzie,

S.J., and Prof. Frederick C. Grant in *The Documents of Vatican II*.

2. Formulate your ideas of revelation, Scripture, tradition, the Church, authority—then discuss with other Christians on a laymen's basis (with or without clergy included).

3. Secure the views of the Eastern Orthodox on these same subjects.

4. Examine a copy of the new Catholic Revised Standard Version Bible.

5. Use the new Catholic Revised Standard Version Bible either at a living-room dialogue session or at an ecumenical prayer service.

"Everywhere, large numbers have felt the impulse of this grace, and among our separated brethren also there increases from day to day a movement, fostered by the grace of the Holy Spirit, for the restoration of unity among all Christians. Taking part in this movement, which is called ecumenical, are those who invoke the Triune God and confess Jesus as Lord and Savior. They join in not merely as individuals but also as members of the corporate groups in which they have heard the gospel, and which each regards as his Church and, indeed, God's. And yet, almost everyone, though in different ways, longs that there may be one visible Church of God, a Church truly universal and sent forth to the whole world that the world may be converted to the gospel and so be saved, to the glory of God." (From the Introduction of the Decree on Ecumenism.)

# CHAPTER IV

# New Ecumenical Relations

## INTRODUCTION

The key document, as far as the ecumenical dialogue is concerned, is the Decree on Ecumenism (*Unitatis Redintegratio*) promulgated by Pope Paul VI "together with the Fathers of the sacred council" on Saturday, November 21, 1964. In this document the Roman Catholic Church goes on record officially, for the first time in its history, as favoring an active dialogue with Protestant and Orthodox churches. Therefore in a very real sense it represents an end to the Counter-Reformation and a new era of full Christian discussion, understanding, and cooperation.

As a statement made by the Committee on Education for Ecumenism, approved by the Bishop's Commission for Ecumenical Affairs of the National Catholic Welfare Conference and presented at the 63rd Annual Convention of the National Catholic Education Association at Chicago on April 12, 1966, puts it: "The Second Vatican Council, most notably in its Decree on Ecumenism, has summoned every Catholic to help bring about the achievement of Christian unity. For over fifty years other Christian Churches have officially been promoting the search for unity. With the Decree on Ecumenism, the Roman Catholic Church has now fully entered into the ecumenical movement, one of the most important religious movements of our century; and has acknowledged that a basis for the practice of ecumenism already exists through a common profession of faith in Christ and through baptism."

# I. THE NEW ROMAN CATHOLIC POSITION

In the following outline are the main points, in summary fashion, of the Decree on Ecumenism.

The very first sentences of the Introduction are significant in relation to the dialogue on Christian union:

> "Promoting the restoration of unity among all Christians is one of the chief concerns of the Second Sacred Ecumenical Synod of the Vatican. The Church established by Christ the Lord is, indeed, one and unique. Yet many Christian communions present themselves to men as the true heritage of Jesus Christ. To be sure, all proclaim themselves to be disciples of the Lord, but their convictions clash and their paths diverge, as though Christ Himself were divided (cf. 1 Cor. 1:13). Without doubt, this discord openly contradicts the will of Christ, provides a stumbling block to the world, and inflicts damage on the most holy cause of proclaiming the good news to every creature."

Chapter I deals with the Catholic Principles on Ecumenism. It points out that Christ established one and only one Church, and prayed that His disciples might be one. He also founded the Eucharist (Lord's Supper) "by which the unity of the Church is both signified and brought about." (Art. 2.) Moreover, it indicates that from the beginning the Church has experienced certain rifts.

The ecumenical movement, it says, is trying to overcome

such divisions. Then comes a statement which signifies a new development in ecumenical relations as far as the Catholic Church is concerned: "Moreover some, even very many, of the most significant elements or endowments which together go to build up and give life to the Church herself can exist outside the visible boundaries of the Catholic Church: the written word of God; the life of grace; faith, hope, and charity, along with other interior gifts of the Holy Spirit and visible elements. All of these, which come from Christ and lead back to Him, belong by right to the one Church of Christ." (Art. 3.)

It is in baptism, and in the leading of the Holy Spirit, that those outside the Catholic Church find a real measure of salvation in Christ. "It follows that these separated Churches and Communities, though we believe they suffer from defects already mentioned, have by no means been deprived of significance and importance in the mystery of salvation. For the Spirit of Christ has not refrained from using them as means of salvation which derive their efficacy from the very fullness of grace and truth entrusted to the Catholic Church." (Art. 3.)

But it is imperative that we note what directly follows, indicating that the separated churches do not have a full or complete means to salvation. "Nevertheless, our separated brethren, whether considered as individuals or as Communities and Churches, are not blessed with that unity which Jesus Christ wished to bestow on all those whom He has regenerated and vivified into one body and newness of life—that unity which the holy Scriptures and the revered tradition of the Church proclaim." (Art. 3.) Then it goes on to say: "For it is through Christ's Catholic Church alone, which is the all-embracing means of salvation, that the fullness of the means of salvation can be obtained. It was to the apostolic college alone, of which Peter is the head, that we believe our Lord entrusted all the blessings of the New Covenant, in order to establish on earth the one Body of Christ into which all those should be fully incorporated who already belong in any way to God's People." (Art. 3.)

On the above basis the Decree proceeds to instruct all members of the Catholic Church to take "an active and intelligent part" in the work of ecumenism. Moreover, it asks Catholics not only to prove the ecumenical spirit by their friendly and Christian behavior, but also to acknowledge and esteem "the truly Christian endowments from our common heritage which are to be found among our separated brethren." (Art. 4.) Catholics, it says, should not forget that anything wrought by the grace of the Holy Spirit in the hearts of "our separated brethren" can contribute to their own edification.

In Chapter II of the document the practice of ecumenism is spelled out in detail. After indicating that Church renewal has notable ecumenical importance and that there can be no ecumenism worthy of the name without interior conversion, it then gives these guidelines to ecumenical action:

1. Under certain special circumstances, such as in prayer services "for unity," and during ecumenical gatherings, it is not only allowable but desirable that Catholics should join in prayer with their separated brethren.

2. Catholics are asked to study the respective doctrines of the separated brethren—their history, spiritual and liturgical life, religious psychology, and cultural background.

3. Discussion groups (dialogues) are favored, provided that those who take part in them have the guidance of competent Catholic authorities.

4. When taking part in a dialogue, Catholic belief, however, must be explained profoundly and precisely, in such a way, and in such terms, that the separated brethren can also truly understand it.

5. The teaching of sacred theology and other branches of knowledge must be taught with due regard to the ecumenical point of view.

6. In dialogue, which is to be conducted in love and with understanding, a "fraternal rivalry" will be created in which a deeper realization and a clearer expression of the unfathomable riches of Christ may be experienced on both sides.

7. Because cooperation in social matters is widespread today and when all men without exception are called to work together, Catholics are urged, in Christ's name, to work with other Christians in such areas as world peace, the application of the Gospel to social life, and in the advancement of the arts and sciences. It should also be intensified "in the use of every possible means to relieve the afflictions of our times, such as famine and natural disasters, illiteracy and poverty, lack of housing, and the unequal distribution of wealth. Through such cooperation, all believers in Christ are able to learn easily how they can

understand each other and esteem each other more, and how the road to the unity of Christians may be made smooth." (Ch. II, Art. 12.)

Chapter III is divided into two sections: the Special Position of the Eastern Churches and the Separated Churches and Ecclesial Communities in the West.

For historical and doctrinal reasons the Eastern churches are given special consideration. "It is equally worthy of note that from their very origins the Churches of the East have had a treasury from which the Church of the West has amply drawn for its liturgy, spiritual tradition, and jurisprudence. Nor must we underestimate the fact that basic dogmas of the Christian faith concerning the Trinity and God's Word made flesh of the Virgin Mary were defined in Ecumenical Councils held in the East. To preserve this faith, these Churches have suffered much, and still do so." (Ch. III, Art. 14.)

Taking this common background into account, Catholics are asked to consider, when working for a reconciliation between the East and the West, that the Eastern churches have a special love for the Sacred Liturgy, the Eucharist, and the Virgin Mary ("whom the Ecumenical Synod of Ephesus solemnly proclaimed to be" the holy Mother of God). "Although these Churches are separated from us, they possess true sacraments, above all—by apostolic succession—the priesthood and the Eucharist, whereby they are still joined to us in a very close relationship. Therefore, given suitable circumstances and the approval of Church authority, some worship in common is not merely possible but is recommended." (Art. 15.)

Therefore the Eastern churches now separated from Rome are considered to be in a special ecclesiastical category. Even though they have their own disciplines, these are "far from being an obstacle to the Church's unity." (Art. 16.) Such diversity of customs and observances "only adds to her comeliness, and contributes greatly to carrying out her mission."

> "To remove any shadow of doubt, then, this sacred Synod solemnly declares that the Churches of the East, while keeping in mind the necessary unity of the whole Church, have the power to govern themselves according to their own disciplines, since these are better suited to the temperament of their faithful and

better adapted to foster the good of souls. Although it has not always been honored, the strict observance of this traditional principle is among the prerequisites for any restoration of unity." (Art. 16.)

What applies to disciplines also applies to differences in theological expressions of doctrine. Various theological formulations are "to be considered often as complementary rather than conflicting." (Art. 17.) Moreover, the Decree calls attention to the fact that members of Eastern Orthodox churches are living in full communion with Christ, and that every effort should be made toward the gradual realization of unity. The Council "hopes that with the removal of the wall dividing the Eastern and Western Church there may at last be but the one dwelling, firmly established on the cornerstone, Christ Jesus, who will make both one." (Art. 18.)

In the second section of Chapter III, dealing with the separated churches of the West, it is stated that whereas there are "very weighty differences" between these churches and the Catholic Church—of a historical, sociological, psychological, and cultural character and "especially in the interpretation of revealed truth"—there are also some factors which serve as a basis and as an encouragement to true dialogue.

The Bible is an important factor in ecumenical relations. "Nevertheless, in dialogue itself, the sacred utterances are precious instruments in the mighty hand of God for attaining that unity which the Savior holds out to all men." (Art. 21.) Baptism is also a bond of Christian unity within the entire Church. "Baptism, therefore, constitutes a sacramental bond of unity linking all who have been reborn by means of it." (Art. 22.)

Although from the Catholic point of view the Eucharist (Lord's Supper) is not celebrated in all its fullness by Protestants, including Anglicans, and although there is "the lack of the sacrament of orders," nevertheless there is in the celebration of the Eucharist a real bond of union in the living Christ. "When they commemorate the Lord's death and resurrection in the Holy Supper, they profess that it signifies life in communion with Christ and they await His coming in glory. For these reasons, dialogue should be undertaken concerning the true meaning of the

Lord's Supper, the other sacraments, and the Church's worship and ministry." (Art. 22.)

Moreover, the unity expressed in Christian living is of vast importance, and this faith by which all real Christians believe in Christ bears fruit not only in praise and thanksgiving, but also in a lively sense of justice and true charity toward others.

> "And if in moral matters there are many Christians who do not always understand the gospel in the same way as Catholics, and do not admit the same solutions for the more difficult problems of modern society, nevertheless they share our desire to cling to Christ's word as the source of Christian virtue and to obey the apostolic command: 'Whatever you do in word or in work, do all in the name of the Lord Jesus, giving thanks to God the Father through him' (Col. 3:17). Hence, the ecumenical dialogue could start with discussions concerning the application of the gospel to moral questions." (Art. 23.)

The Decree on Ecumenism closes with a forward look, indicating that only a beginning has been made in ecumenical relations and that all Christians should press forward toward that fullness in which Christ wants his Church to grow in the course of time. Therefore the Council "urgently desires that the initiatives of the sons of the Catholic Church, joined with those of the separated brethren, go forward without obstructing the ways of divine Providence, and without prejudging the future inspiration of the Holy Spirit." (Art. 24.)

## II. PROTESTANT AND ORTHODOX POSITIONS

Dr. Robert McAfee Brown, on the day (November 18, 1963) when the Decree on Ecumenism was officially "launched in rough seas," wrote in his diary, "Today is a historic day in Roman Catholic history, and indeed in ecumenical history. This morning, for the first time in four hundred years, the Roman Catholic Church has initiated formal discussion of its relation to divided Christendom. Pere Congar's comment before Mass was significant: 'This is the day for which we have been waiting for many decades.' He should know, better than most, for it was his pioneering book on ecumenism, suppressed by the Holy Office, that began to focus Catholic attention on the problem." (*Observer in Rome,* Doubleday, p. 139.)

Protestant observers on the whole received this Decree with special enthusiasm, for it represented not only a change in direction and attitude toward non-Catholics but also a vindication of the long, hard, and creative labors of the Secretariat for the Promotion of Christian Unity and its President, Augustin Cardinal Bea. It made the very presence of the official observers at the Council of real significance. It indicated that they were no longer outsiders looking on, but separated brethren invited to observe progress being made in a common cause—that of Christian unity. This was expressed by Dr. Oscar Cullmann, Protestant scholar and guest-observer at the Second Vatican Council, when he said directly after the Decree on Ecumenism was promulgated, "The schema on ecumenism, which has been accepted by a surprisingly large majority—the very numbers show that a door has been opened—is not just a text, but an ecumenical deed. In fact, this is more than the opening of a door: new ground has been broken. No Catholic document has ever spoken of non-Catholic Christians in this way. Every single chapter of this schema bears witness of this. . . ." (Quoted in *A Stand on Ecumenism: The Council's Decree,* by Lorenz Cardinal Jaeger, J. J. Kenedy & Sons, 1965.)

Methodist Bishop Fred Pierce Corson of Philadelphia probably sums up the majority feeling of the Protestant and Orthodox observers when he says in a television dialogue with Archbishop John J. Krol, "When I told the Holy Father [Pope John XXIII] that unity for him and for me was already in our hearts, for us unity had already been accomplished."

Here is pointed up both the real meaning of the word "ecumenical" and the nature of a united Church. Although there is now an ecumenical movement in which Protestants, Catholics, and Orthodox are actively engaged, this does not mean that the Council proposed any steps toward organic union. There are certain movements in the direction of unity, particularly in relation to the Orthodox churches but these are more in the form of friendly gestures and the expression of a willingness to cooperate. In regard to the issue of Church union itself, no specific plan has been developed. In fact, some leading churchmen have raised the question whether Catholics and Orthodox, and Protestants, are talking about the same thing when they use the word "ecumenical." To some it apparently means a return to the one true Church; to others it means a new reform and renewed Church, of a much higher institutional and spiritual nature, to which all three faiths will give their allegiance.

After giving the decree a very careful analysis, both pro and con, Dr. Edmund Schlink, Professor of Systematic Theology at the University of Heidelberg, Germany, says, "No matter what our final judgment may be, the Decree on Ecumenism of the Second Vatican Council is so important that no church can pass it by. It has brought about a new relationship between the Roman Church and the other churches. Every church will have to study it carefully and will gratefully acknowledge the possibilities which this decree opens up for the future." (*Dialogue on the Way*, Augsburg Publishing House, 1965.) What the future holds in store for the Church no one knows. Yet it is even now certain, because of this Decree on Ecumenism, that the Church can never be the same as it has been.

In regard to the Eastern Orthodox position: although there are certain differences and particular emphases within the Orthodox churches, there has been on the whole a special welcome and a deep sense of appreciation for the Decree on Ecumenism. Outwardly this attitude has been expressed in two historic occasions, the meeting of Pope Paul VI with Patriarch Athenagoras in the Holy Land, and the mutual cancellation of the excommunications imposed upon the heads of each body (Roman Catholic and Eastern Orthodox) growing out of the split of 1054 A.D.

The Orthodox churches are closely allied to the Roman Catholic Church in doctrine and practice, holding similar positions in regard to the Sacraments, the Eucharist, Orders, the Scriptures, and the Virgin Mary.

Professor Ioannidis of the theological faculty of the University of Athens has described the likeness of Orthodoxy to the Roman Catholic Church as follows: "While our differences from the Roman Catholics are very few, the links that bind us together are very many and of substantial importance. We constitute with them in fact one family because we have the same sources of faith—

Holy Scripture and Holy Tradition—the same Fathers, the same Saints, the same Apostolic succession in the episcopal dignity, the same seven sacraments, the same holy worship, the same monastic and ascetical life, and the same understanding of the church as the Body of Christ, as visible and invisible, although their views about the primacy have added a different emphasis to Roman Catholic opinions about the church." (From *Catholic and Orthodox Can They Unite?*, by Clement C. Englert, C.SS.R., Paulist Press.)

The problems of Christian union are many and varied, and they are emphasized in a most realistic manner in the Decree on Ecumenism. Although it represented a major step forward in ecumenical relations, it also stated dogmatically several propositions which few Protestants are willing to accept at face value.

For example, at the very beginning, the sentence, "Christ the Lord founded one Church and one Church only" is open to serious question particularly when it (a) is meant to apply to the Roman Catholic Church only and (b) when it places the non-Catholic churches in a position of being outside the kind of Church which Christ meant to establish.

In Chapter I, first paragraph, there is the sentence "In His Church He instituted the wonderful sacrament of the Eucharist by which the unity of the Church is both signified and brought about." This of course opens several basic issues dealing with the nature of the Lord's Supper as a "sacrament" and what is known as the "real presence." Moreover, the whole question of the Mass raises major theological questions in the minds of most Protestants.

This is also true of the primacy of the Pope. The dialogue will focus on the validity of Peter's appointment as the first Pope, as well as upon such matters as papal infallibility and apostolic succession (Orders).

While it is pleasing to many ecumenically minded Protestants to learn that "men who believe in Christ and have been properly baptized are brought into certain, though imperfect, communion with the Catholic Church" (Ch. I, Art. 3), the whole issue of the validity of baptism still remains as an issue. Several major denominations will not accept the proposition that the sacrament of baptism is a "saving rite" imparting supernatural grace. These denominations accept baptism as an example, as an ordinance, as an initiation into the Church following a personal rebirth in Christ.

In the dialogue the whole question of the validity of baptism, its meaning, its relationship to Church membership and to "original sin," and its form, will have to come up for discussion. At a time when infant baptism is being questioned by scholars and priests alike, it also will have to be examined both in relation to New Testament teaching and in respect to modern demands upon members of the Church.

Near the end of the Decree on Ecumenism (Ch. III, Art. 21) there is one word which is causing Protestants much difficulty. It is the word "seek." In the text submitted to the Council for final consideration the sentence read: "While invoking the Holy Spirit, they [the separated brethren] *find* in these very Scriptures God as He speaks to them in Christ, the One whom the prophets foretold, the Word of God made flesh for us."

Pope Paul VI at the very last moment added nineteen amendments to the text. One of these changed "find" to "seek." According to Father Thomas F. Stransky, in his commentary on the Decree on Ecumenism (*Study-Club Edition: The Decree on Ecumenism*, Deus Books, Paulist Press, p. 79), "The change was made, it seems, in order to avoid a possible implication that the Decree approves of the *direct* individual inspiration of the Holy Spirit in the *private* and infallible interpretation of Scriptures. Such a theory would make the teaching authority or magisterium of the Church objectively superfluous." Yet it is the position of Protestantism that the Holy Spirit, directly or speaking through Scripture, does reach the individual on a personal basis; the individual does not have to get his interpretation through the Church. Here is another basic issue upon which new light will have to be focused in the dialogue.

The part of the Decree on Ecumenism which troubles Protestants perhaps the most is the following paragraph which appears in Chapter I, Article 3, of the document:

> "Nevertheless, our separated brethren, whether considered as individuals or as Communities and Churches, are not blessed with that unity which Jesus Christ wished to bestow on all those to whom He has regenerated and vivified into one body and

newness of life—that unity which the Holy Scriptures and the revered tradition of the Church proclaim. For it is through Christ's Catholic Church alone, which is the all-embracing means of salvation, that the fullness of the means of salvation can be obtained. It was to the apostolic college alone, of which Peter is the head, that we believe that our Lord entrusted all the blessings of the New Covenant, in order to establish on earth the one Body of Christ into which all those should be fully incorporated who already belong in any way to God's People."

If this means what it appears to say, then Protestants—if they are to be true to their Protestant heritage—will have to reject the basic premises proclaimed therein. Because most Protestants already feel that they are a true and real part of the Christian Church, as established by Christ, and that their denominations, although all too human, are within the framework of the visible Church. This does not mean that there is no possibility of improving the Protestant churches, or even uniting in a new Church, built more solidly on New Testament foundations, sometime in the future. Relatively few Protestants will admit, as of the present, that their churches are lacking in grace or that they are not fully Christian. They do not consider themselves second-class Christians.

What many (probably the majority of Protestants) will admit is this: that they are still pilgrims on the way to greater spiritual achievement and that their churches are pilgrim churches moving forward toward perpetual reform and continual renewal. It is at this point that the Decree on Ecumenism holds forth a hope and a promise. For it does stress reform and renewal (Chapter II); it does leave the door open to something new and better as far as the physical, visible, all-too-human institutional Church (Chapter III) is concerned. As the Catholic theologian Hans Küng stresses, if all Christians and all Christian bodies move forward through the New Testament to Christ Himself, then in time (perhaps a very long time) all of us will be brought together in Christ. What this means in relation to a new reborn Church, somewhere out in the future, of course nobody knows. But it does challenge the imagination; it does present a challenge to all the churches.

As has already been noted, the relationship to Eastern Orthodox churches, because of common history, worship, and ecclesiastical aspects, is different and in some respects much closer than the relationship to Protestant bodies. Therefore this difference has to be taken into consideration when making this appraisal of the Decree on Ecumenism by Christians outside the Roman Catholic fold. The Roman Catholic Church and the Orthodox churches have their major points of difference. In the Orthodox communions there is no single head; the Ecumenical Patriarch of Constantinople is given an honorary preference, "a priority of respect," but it does not give him authority or universal jurisdiction over any of the other heads of Orthodox churches which are usually of a national character. There are basic differences not only between the Orthodox and the Catholic churches on the nature of the Church and the primacy of the Pope, but between Orthodox and Protestants on such matters of doctrine as the seven sacraments, orders, and the missionary enterprise. There are also differences in regard to the purpose and direction of the ecumenical movement. Despite the fact that the Orthodox Church plays a leading role in the World Council of Churches (while the Roman Catholic Church is not a member of the Council),[1] nevertheless it claims to be the only one true Church (as the Roman Catholic Church also claims to be).

After reviewing recent events in the ecumenical movement sympathetically, Father George Florovsky, a leading scholar of the Orthodox Church, says, "Personally I am not looking forward to any spectacular events in the ecumenical field in the near future. Nor am I interested in the official negotiations concerning unity or reunion. There is much work to be done on the more intimate level and in an informal way. And this work must be done. There is an urgency and there is a promise. But the advance is in the hands of the Lord." (*Ecumenical Experiences,* edited by Luis V. Romeu, London, Burns & Oates, p. 45.)

---

[1] On December 3, 1966, the Roman Catholic Church was made eligible for a policy-making role in the National Council of Churches. For the previous two years, it held observer status. The action provides that in areas where it chooses to become involved, the Catholic Church will be eligible to have representations on policy-making boards and committees and to provide full-time staff personnel. It will also be entitled to send non-voting fraternal delegates to the triennial general assembly, the council's highest policy-making body.

# III. QUESTIONS FOR DISCUSSION

1. What is meant by the word "ecumenical"?

2. Why is the Decree on Ecumenism such an important "breakthrough"?

3. How far does the Roman Catholic Church now go in ecumenical relations?

4. What areas of difficulty still remain in the area of ecumenical understanding and action?

5. In what sense does the Roman Catholic Church claim to be the one and only true Church?

6. Why does the Eastern Orthodox Church also claim to be the one and only true Church?

7. What keeps the Roman Catholic Church and the Eastern Orthodox Church from reuniting?

8. Should Catholics, Protestants, and the Orthodox aim to have one organic institution?

9. At what points can all three faiths cooperate?

10. How can the three faiths demonstrate to the world that they support together such great causes as world peace, the war against poverty, and better race relations?

# IV. SUGGESTIONS FOR ECUMENICAL ACTION

1. Read carefully the Decree on Ecumenism as found in *The Documents of Vatican II.*

2. Establish dialogue centers in your immediate community or church using this book as a discussion guide.

3. Unite with Protestant, Catholic, and Orthodox churches in ecumenical prayer services during such times as the Week of Prayer for Christian Unity and at special ecumenical services.

4. Exchange visits with a church (or members of another faith), as far as this is allowed.

5. Create and participate in local or area conferences on ecumenical relations sponsored by church groups, Y.M.C.A., Y.W.C.A., etc.

7. Challenge biased statements found in newspapers, magazines, or over radio-TV. (A letter to the editor or manager can often do a lot of good.)

8. Encourage your church to produce radio and television programs of an ecumenical nature.

9. Make sure that the teaching materials in the church which you attend are a hundred percent ecumenical.

10. Start a circulating library of books dealing with the whole ecumenical field. (See bibliography at the end of this volume.) Also get your church and public library to secure such books.

11. Check the public school system to make sure that it is fair to all religious faiths, within the principle of the separation of Church and State.

# PART TWO

# *Implementation:*
# *Out in the Modern World*

"It would have been possible for the Second Vatican Council to concern itself solely with internal affairs—the reform of the liturgy, a fresh look at seminary education, and so on—and it is highly significant that rather than doing so the Council also turned outward to examine the ways in which a Church subject to 'reform and renewal' should relate to those beyond its walls."

> —*Dr. Robert McAfee Brown in a Response to the Pastoral Constitution on the Church in the Modern World in* The Documents of Vatican II *(p. 309).*

". . . the conviction grows not only that humanity can and should increasingly consolidate its control over creation, but even more, that it devolves on humanity to establish a political, social, and economic order which will to an ever better extent serve men and help individuals as well as groups to affirm and develop the dignity proper to them." (Intro., Art. 9.)

". . . in the face of the modern development of the world, an ever-increasing number of people are raising the most basic questions or recognizing them with a new sharpness: what is man? What is this sense of sorrow, of evil, of death, which continues to exist despite so much progress? What is the purpose of these victories, purchased at so high a cost? What can man offer to society, what can he expect from it? What follows this earthly life?" (Intro., Art. 10.)

"The Church believes that Christ, who died and was raised up for all, can through His Spirit offer man the light and the strength to measure up to his supreme destiny." (Intro., Art. 10.)

". . . Hence in the light of Christ, the image of the unseen God, the firstborn of every creature, the Council wishes to speak to all men in order to illuminate the mystery of man and to cooperate in finding the solution to the outstanding problems of our time." (Intro., Art. 10.)

## CHAPTER V

# Ministry to the World

## INTRODUCTION

The Pastoral Constitution on the Church in the Modern World (*Gaudium et Spes*) was promulgated by Pope Paul VI on December 7, 1965. It confronts us with two miracles. The major one is that a church which a hundred years ago under Pius IX feared and fought the world and its culture now faces it with confidence and with benevolence. The minor one is that a declaration which began as an afterthought, developed by confusing accretion, and attained assured form and status only in the closing days of the Council, has said so much that is helpful on the most perplexing and controversial matters, and—in laying down principles—has achieved a majestic sweep that makes it a worthy complement to the great Dogmatic Constitution on the Church.

Timid at some points, incomplete at some, it is frankly open-ended. It prepares the way for Christian dialogue, intramural and ecumenical, and for extra-ecclesial conversation. The impression it leaves on the reader is less monopolistic, less condescending, than that of Pope Paul's encyclical letter (Aug. 6, 1964) *Ecclesiam Suam,* which seemed more ready to teach than to learn.

There were times when it seemed that it would be impossible to make a Constitution of the miscellany. At the end of the third session, half of the material had not been digested by the mixed commission, and was laid before the bishops as supplementary "annexes." There were friendly proposals to issue a collegial message, or to refer the proposals to the new Bishops' Synod as its first agenda. Later, the opposition seized on the message idea as a means of postponing, defeating, or downgrading Schema XIII (formerly XVII), and it became clear that nothing less than a Constitution would carry the required emphasis and dignity.

# I. SUMMARY OF THE PASTORAL CONSTITUTION

After expressing in the Preface the solidarity of "the followers of Christ" (Art. 1) with all men, especially the poor, the Council, "having probed more profoundly into the mystery of the Church, now addresses itself without hesitation, not only to the sons of the Church and to all who invoke the name of Christ, but to the whole of humanity." (Art. 2.) In Article 3, the Council speaks in the name of "the whole People of God," tying this Pastoral Constitution even more closely to the Dogmatic Constitution on the Church.

We note that the Council can speak with more grace and more plausibility to "the whole of humanity," having already promulgated the Decrees on Ecumenism and on the Non-Christian Religions.

We note also that with each extension of the Church's interest and appeal, it becomes more difficult to give "ecumenism" a precise meaning, and to distinguish Christian, Judeo-Christian, theistic, and inter-religious uses of the word and the concept.

The Introductory Statement (Articles 4-10), on the situation of men in the modern world, presents fairly and vigorously the challenge of the rapid changes, growing imbalances, and lethal conflicts of today's world to humanity itself as well as to religion. Scientism, depersonalization, increase of the migratory population, undermining of the family, go along with the many material and intellectual elements of progress.

From these articles we have taken the quotations that head this chapter. Along with a new and renewed acceptance of the modern challenge, they indicate renewed confidence in the gospel's response to the challenge.

## PART I: THE CHURCH AND MAN'S CALLING.
Article 11 is headed: The Impulses of the Spirit Demand a Response. "The People of God believes that it is led by the Spirit of the Lord who fills the earth."

"What is the ultimate significance of human activity throughout the world? . . . it will be increasingly clear that the People of God and the human race in whose midst it lives render service to each other. Thus the mission of the Church will show its religious, and by that very fact, its supremely human character."

Chapter I concerns *the dignity of the human person.* Man, made "to the image of God" (Art. 12), is by his innermost nature a social being; the primary instance is the "interpersonal communion" of male and female.

"Although he was made by God in a state of holiness, from the very dawn of history man abused his liberty, at the urging of personified Evil." A less rigid biblically founded statement of the doctrine of original sin would be hard to formulate. The Council tries hard in this Constitution to employ a language—biblical but not scholastic— usable in dialogue with the secular world. "For sin has diminished man, blocking his path to fulfillment." "But the

Lord Himself came to free and strengthen man, renewing him inwardly and casting out that prince of this world." (Art. 13.)

Man is one, body and soul. "Man is not wrong when he regards himself as superior to bodily concerns, and as more than a speck of nature or a nameless constituent of the city of man." (Art. 14.)

To his intellectual capacity for discovering truth, man must add wisdom—more than formerly, if he is to humanize his discoveries: "the future of the world stands in peril unless wiser men are forthcoming." (Art. 15.) The help of the Holy Spirit is required, if human plans are to fit the divine plan.

Articles 16 and 17 on the dignity of the moral conscience and the excellence of liberty might well be read in connection with the Declaration on Religious Freedom, and would fit well there, since it also is based on the dignity of man.

"In the depths of his conscience, man detects a law which he does not impose upon himself, but which holds him to obedience. . . . Conscience is the most secret core and sanctuary of a man. There he is alone with God. . . ." (Art. 16.)

"Only in freedom can man direct himself toward goodness . . . authentic freedom is an exceptional sign of the divine image within man. . . . Since man's freedom has been damaged by sin, only by the help of God's grace can he bring such a relationship with God into full flower." (Art. 17.)

Article 18 on the mystery of death is moving and profound. Christianity's answer to the riddle which "utterly beggars the imagination" explains nothing to the intellectual: to Christian and humanist it offers the faith made believable by the Church's witness to Christ's resurrection, and the inextinguishable belief that man "bears in himself an eternal seed which cannot be reduced to sheer matter."

One who accepts the last affirmation (with or without belief in the resurrection) will find it hard to be an atheist —having already admitted an element of transcendence. Not inappropriately, a discussion of atheism occupies the three articles between the subject of death and "Christ as the new man."

A principal source and support of man's dignity is his

"call to communion with God." (Art. 19.) But not all men recognize this, and their atheism takes diverse forms. Some atheists over-exalt man more than they deny God. Some deny a God who is not the one to be found in the gospel. Christians sometimes share the blame for the creation of such false ideas of God. But "those who willfully shut out God from their hearts and try to dodge religious questions are not following the dictates of their consciences. Hence they are not free of blame." (Art. 19.) One is struck, however, not only by the absence of anathemas (which absence is notable in the Council deliberations and documents, as Pope John desired), but by the evident desire to understand and the feeling of compassion.

There is a contemporary atheism that finds man's freedom inconsistent with dependence on God. The feeling of self-sufficiency is stimulated by man's technical achievements. Conversely, dependence on God is held to weaken man's own striving and creativity. "Consequently, when the proponents of this doctrine gain governmental power they vigorously fight against religion. They promote atheism by using those means of pressure which public power has at its disposal. Such is especially the case in the work of educating the young." (Art. 20.) In spite of the clear-cut repudiation of atheism in power in this and other passages, there was a determined effort by three or four hundred bishops, from many lands, to have the Council anathematize communism. In a few places, anti-communism is doubtless a test and a trademark of Christian alignment, and failure to condemn it generically and by name would be felt by Christian pastors (rightly or wrongly) as a handicap. But a wholesale condemnation of a communism that is changing into as many diverse forms (almost) as Christianity itself would have been highly confusing, and out of tone with the Constitution's whole approach to dialogue and understanding—and by no means favorable to the search for peace. Consistent, in this sense, is the statement in Article 21 that the Church "strives to detect in the atheistic mind the hidden causes of the denial of God. Conscious of how weighty are the questions which atheism raises, and motivated by love for all men, she believes these questions ought to be examined seriously and more profoundly."

Only God, we are told, supplies the answer; this can

be done in part through "a proper presentation of the Church's teaching as well as in the integral life of the Church and her members, . . . led by the Holy Spirit."

The Constitution invites atheists into dialogue for cooperation in useful enterprises, and "protests against the distinction which some state authorities unjustly make," barring believers from cooperation.

In Article 22 Christ is presented not only as the answer to atheism but as the key to the mystery of man. Incarnate Word, "He merited life for us by the free shedding of His own blood. . . . He blazed a trail, and if we follow it, life and death are made holy and take on a new meaning." . . . "All this holds true not only for Christians, but for all men of good will in whose hearts grace works in an unseen way" through the help of "the Holy Spirit in a manner known only to God." Here again one seems to encounter biblical faith without the strait-jacket of a syllogistic theology.

Chapter II (on the community of mankind) especially, and the Constitution generally, draw heavily on Pope John's great encyclicals, *Mater et Magistra* and *Pacem in Terris*.

Men's growing interdependence, aided by technology, calls for dialogue on the deeper level of interpersonal relationships. "Love of God cannot be separated from love of neighbor." (Art. 24.) It is unusual, but cogent, to have Jn. 17:21-22 cited on behalf of the unity of all mankind —of which, no doubt, Christian unity is the preparation, and to which it may be an indispensable approach. Likewise, as Article 25 points out, the path to God leads through society—a place both of development and of testing.

Articles 26 and 27 point out how much work will be required if society is to be the servant of man, minister to his dignity; they list a score of obstacles in the path of reverence for the human person. The next article shows both the need and the possibility of reverence and love for those who oppose us—in no wise indifferent to the truth and goodness that they may betray: "love itself impels the disciples of Christ to speak the saving truth to all men."

Men's equality before God requires social justice for all. "Excessive economic and social differences" (Art. 29) in the human family or in a given society militate against justice, human dignity, social and international peace.

Many show little consideration for the requirements of society, not only ignoring but actually violating them. Rather than calling for penalties, the Constitution appeals to them in the name of their sacred obligation to a needy humanity, and for the creation, with the help of divine grace, of a new humanity.

This calls also for education, and education is sorely handicapped for those living in conditions that deny human dignity and limit freedom of choice and opportunity. "Praise is due to those national procedures which allow the largest possible number of citizens to participate in public affairs with genuine freedom." (Art. 31.)

The chapter concludes with Christ's own encouragement, by example and by preaching, to human solidarity.

Chapter III is titled Man's Activity Throughout the World. Men by their research and industry have now available many blessings which they once could expect only from heaven. But they are asking what is the real use and meaning of their feverish activity and achievements. The Church does not claim to have a ready answer to all such questions.

But it holds that even the humblest necessary activity accords with God's will: man is neither His foe nor rival in His creativity. Yet the material riches man creates are not as important as his own growth that takes place in the process of his work for the benefit of others.

Nor is religion in conflict with the independence that is essential to man's development. Thus the scientist is not inhibited. Science too depends on God's laws. "Indeed, whoever labors to penetrate the secrets of reality with a humble and steady mind, is, even unawares, being led by the hand of God, who holds all things in existence, and gives them their identity." (Art. 36.)

This article accords well with repeated expressions in and around the Council that "one Galileo case is enough!" In fact, Pope Paul, deftly and rather unobtrusively in a speech in Pisa, "rehabilitated" Galileo, and is supporting the publication of a book favorable to him.

Progress brings temptations toward selfish enjoyment or power, calling for God's grace. Christ's example of sacrificial love is of the utmost significance here.

(Note: Some who were dismayed by the manner and timing of Pope Paul's encyclical on transubstantiation will be struck by the Council's phrase in Article 38, "elements

. . . changed into His glorified Body and Blood. . . .")

The concluding article (39) is a biblically grounded forecast of "a new earth and a new heaven," which, the Council held, will conserve and transmute the values that men shall have acquired.

Chapter IV takes up the role of the Church in the modern world. "That the earthly and the heavenly city penetrate each other is a fact accessible to faith alone." "Through her individual members and her whole community, the Church believes she can contribute greatly toward making the family of man and its history more human." (Art. 40.)

Through the constant working of God's spirit on men, "the Church can anchor the dignity of human nature against all tides of opinion. . . ." "By virtue of the gospel committed to her, the Church proclaims the rights of man." (Art. 41.) Without the gospel, human strivings are in danger of assuming a false autonomy.

"Christ, to be sure, gave His Church no proper mission in the political, economic, or social order. The purpose which He set before her is a religious one. But out of this religious mission itself come a function, a light, and an energy which can serve to structure and consolidate the human community according to the divine law. As a matter of fact, when circumstances of time and place create the need, she can and indeed should initiate activities on behalf of all men. This is particularly true of activities designed for the needy, such as the works of mercy and similar undertakings." (Art. 42.)

". . . she [the Church] is bound to no particular form of human culture, nor to any political, economic, or social system." By strong inference, this article, 42, puts the Church, in the Council's view, on the side of "peaceful coexistence."

Article 43 asserts that men are citizens of two cities and interest in the celestial does not justify shirking their duties in the terrestrial one. Both the Old Testament prophets and Christ inveigh against the split between the professed faith and the daily life. Laymen bear a special responsibility to work "with men seeking the same goals," and unhesitatingly to devise new enterprises, and make their faith effective in secular life. They should become experts, not expecting such specialized service from their ministers. They cannot indeed cite the Church's authority to decide controversies where there are legitimate differences. The article connects significantly with the Dogmatic Constitution on the Church, both in appealing to the laity and in laying down the duty of bishops to study, preach, and administer so as to promote human welfare and unity. The past inadequacy of the Church is acknowledged, though not with details.

The Church recognizes a debt to social and scientific advances. She understands man better. She can adapt her message more effectively to men's understanding and needs. This acknowledgment, in Article 44, of the need and possibility to adapt the Christian message is at the very heart of *aggiornamento*.

The Christian goal is the coming of God's kingdom; the Church is " 'the universal sacrament of salvation' " (Art. 45) (drawing again on the Dogmatic Constitution). The mission is symbolized and vitalized by Christ, the Alpha and Omega.

**PART II: SOME PROBLEMS OF SPECIAL URGENCY.** Chapter I, on fostering the nobility of marriage and the family, is remarkable for what it says in support and guidance of marriage, while not dealing directly with birth control. For advice on that subject, Pope Paul created a special commission including scientists and other lay people. The commission proved unable to agree—it has been reported that the chief differences were among the men of science—and the Pope reorganized it. In enumerating modern problems connected with the family, "world problems resulting from population growth" (Art. 47) are included.

In spite of difficulties, "the power and strength of the institution of marriage and family" have been revealed time and again. Chapter I undertakes to present only "certain key points of Church doctrine in a clearer light" to aid "Christians and other men" (Art. 47) who are trying to maintain the sacredness and dignity of marriage.

In a strong article (48) on the sanctity of marriage and the family, and elsewhere in the Constitution, the Council notably avoids naming procreation as the primary end (or sole justification!) of marriage as many traditionalists would have preferred. There were strong protests in discussions in and around St. Peter's against reducing human marriage to the animal level. In this article, the relation between human and divine love, the obligation to children, and the contribution made to the home by the children are well developed.

The whole Constitution deals far more with persons in society and with personal problems than with society as an impersonal mass. This emphasis is conspicuous in the article on conjugal love (49), which in large part echoes and develops a passage in Pius XI's encyclical, *Casti Connubii* of 1930. "This love is uniquely expressed and perfected" through the mutual giving of themselves by the spouses in the marital act. Marriage was "firmly established by the Lord." The contrast with "mere erotic inclination" is underscored.

In Article 50 on the fruitfulness of marriage, we read that parents, in their "proper mission" of transmitting human life and educating their children, are "cooperators with the love of God the creator. . . . With docile reverence toward God, they will come to the right decision by common counsel and effort." "They will thoughtfully take into account both their own welfare and that of their children, those already born and those which may be foreseen."

In harmonizing conjugal love with respect for human life, "the Church issues the reminder that a true contradiction cannot exist between the divine laws pertaining to the transmission of life and those pertaining to the fostering of authentic conjugal love." (Art. 51.) Pope Paul insisted that this section maintain the teaching of his predecessors; the Council was careful to do this in a way not to prejudice the work of his commission. In an unprecedented newspaper interview in 1965, Pope Paul made clear his perplexity and his sense of ultimate papal responsibility in respect to this subject.

Article 52 exalts the role of the family as a "kind of school of deeper humanity," calling for support and cooperation from all, emphasizing the indispensable "active presence" of the father, and insisting that the mother's "domestic role" must be "safely preserved," though without underrating the "legitimate social progress of women." The article pleads for the education of children for responsible adult life. As the "foundation of society," the family merits the support and protection of public authority, including concern and care for orphans. Various members of society and the Church who can aid family life are named and called upon to do so, including pastors and the spouses themselves.

After introductory definitions and comments, Chapter II, on the proper development of culture, continues with three sections: The Circumstances of Culture in the World Today; Some Principles of Proper Cultural Development; Some Especially Urgent Duties of Christians with Regard to Culture.

In Article 54, attention is called to the effects of "the so-called exact sciences" in sharpening critical judgment, of psychological research in explaining "human activity more profoundly," and of historical studies in "bringing men to see things in their changeable and evolutionary aspects." Communication is helping, little by little, to develop "a more universal form of human culture." As men and women become increasingly conscious artisans and authors of the culture of their community, we witness "the birth of a new humanism," with increased awareness of personhood and of social responsibility. (Art. 55.)

Some problems: how to prevent the universalization of culture from undermining established values of particular cultures; how to synthesize special branches of knowledge and determine where wisdom lies; how to share values during a cultural explosion and avoid a hurtful gap between the mass and the sophisticated elite; how to maintain cultural independence without ignoring or combating religion.

The transcendent character of the Christian's faith increases his "obligation to work with all men in constructing a more human world." (Art. 57.) Thus we find the Roman Catholic Church striving to find the way in which its priests may identify with laborers, and a Protestant Episcopal bishop leaving church administration to represent religious faith and values in an influential creative center for the study of a democratic society.

The danger and dangers of "scientism," leading to agnosticism and supposed human self-sufficiency, do not diminish the achievements and values of science. Among these are fidelity to truth, cooperation—even international—and a sense of responsibility for human welfare.

The gospel can enrich every culture. In the course of conveying its message to people of many languages and customs, the Church probes more deeply into the gospel itself. Thus the gospel civilizes by evangelization—but evangelizing is the primary concern and mission of the Church.

Culture must be free to create its own forms, without interference by religion or politics. It must of course respect individual rights and the common good.

Basic culture (at least) has become a possibility for all, and all men, especially Christians, should work for the political and economic decisions favorable to the wiping out of ignorance. Uneducated individuals are unable to make their potential contribution to the common good. People, both men and women, must be made aware of their right to culture, and helped to pursue higher studies, according to their capacity. To know everything, or to synthesize all knowledge, becomes constantly more difficult for the individual, even as men move toward a universal culture. "It remains each man's duty," aided by the family, "to preserve a view of the whole human person, a view in which the values of intellect, will, conscience, and fraternity are pre-eminent." (Art. 61.) The increase in leisure time facilitates the stimulus and aid that men in association can provide outside the home. Christians have a special responsibility here.

Yet culture and Christian teaching are sometimes hard to harmonize. The difficulties may be made more of a challenge than an obstacle to faith. "Theologians are invited to seek continually for more suitable ways of communicating doctrine to the men of their times. For the deposit of faith or revealed truths are one thing; the manner in which they are formulated without violence to their meaning and significance is another." (Art. 62.) This passage accords well with statements by Pope John, and could be used to counterbalance Pope Paul's somewhat different emphasis in his ringing reaffirmation of the doctrine of transubstantiation. Culture contributes to religion; artists and authors should be made aware of the recognition of the Church. Science, art, morality, and Christian teaching can and should be made to operate in harmony. (This section supports, if it does not supplement, the Decree on Priestly Formation.)

In Chapter III, Socio-Economic Life, the key again is "the dignity and total vocation of the human person." Economic progress has contributed to human values. But many seem to be "hypnotized, as it were, by economics." Affluence could be used to reduce inequalities: "too often it serves only to intensify" them. They exist between the few and the many; between agriculture, industry, and the services; between different areas and nations—to the point of jeopardizing world peace. The "Church maintains certain principles of justice and equity." (Art. 63.) The Council wished to up-date their interpretation and re-enforce them.

Three articles, In the Service of Man (64), Under Man's Control (65), and Removing Huge Differences (66), make up Section 1 (Economic Development) of Chapter II. The whole man, all men. With control involving all interests concerned—local, national, international—not laissez-faire, not solely governmental, not allowing needed resources to be undeveloped. The special needs and rights of farmers and of migrant workers, interregional or international, are emphasized. Automation calls for care "that sufficient and suitable work can be obtained." The section also calls for health protection for workers.

Section 2 covers certain principles governing socio-economic life as a whole. Labor is "superior to the other elements of economic life . . . comes immediately from the person." Jesus Christ worked, "conferred an eminent dignity on labor. . . ." (Art. 67.) Work, for most, helps to support the family. Men have both the duty and the right to work, with protection for health and leisure, and especially in the case of working mothers, for their home life.

Men, working together, have the right of "active participation in the running of an enterprise," and of "freely founding labor unions" truly representing the workers. In economic conflicts, peaceful settlement must be sought, but "even in present-day circumstances, the strike can still be a necessary, though ultimate, means for the defense of the workers' own rights" (Art. 68), but ways should be sought to resume negotiations.

"God intended the earth and all that it contains for the use of every human being and people." A man should regard his possessions "as common property in the sense that they should accrue to the benefit not only of himself but of others." "In extreme necessity, he has the right to take from the riches of others what he himself needs." Some Church Fathers said that not to feed a man dying of hunger is to kill him. Nations must share, particularly the means for helping themselves. Customs provide a degree of mutual care in economically advanced societies; they may need to be adapted as the society develops, but not rashly abandoned. In "highly developed nations . . . institutions dealing with insurance and security" can help to "make the common purpose of earthly goods effective." (Art. 69.)

Fair distribution for the present and planning for the needs of the future are both required, in dealing with both goods and money.

Control of material goods contributes to the expression of personality and is a part of one's freedom; its forms may vary. Private control may be transferred to public control (with which in general it can coexist) only by competent authority. Since private property has a social quality, its selfish use helps to bring the right itself into question. Thus it is wrong to let "gigantic rural estates" be idle or undercultivated for the sake of profit. Nor are hired laborers and tenants "to receive a wage or income unworthy of human beings, to lack decent housing, and to be exploited by middlemen." (Art. 71.) To avoid such abuses, there may even be resort to expropriation—with equitable compensation. "Christians . . . can make a great contribution to the prosperity of mankind and the peace of the world" (Art. 72) by defending justice and charity in such areas, in the spirit of Christ and the gospel.

The life of the political community is the subject of Chapter IV. People more and more are enjoying and demanding civil and religious freedom and respect for minorities which are in turn expected to reciprocate. These developments require "fostering an inner sense of justice, benevolence, and service for the common good," and sound understanding of the "nature of the political community" and "the proper exercise and limits of public authority." (Art. 73.)

The wider community has need of a wider authority than that of the families or other groups that compose it. They must obey that authority whose duty is to serve the common good. If it fails or transgresses, it should still be obeyed as far as the common good demands. It may be resisted when necessary within "the limits imposed by natural law and the gospel." (Art. 74.) This might mean nonviolently.

Article 75 makes clear that the traditional suspicion and fear of democracy are not supported by the Council.

The right and duty to vote are supported. Public service is lauded.

Authorities must not hinder but promote family, social, and cultural groups, and intermediate bodies, in their efforts for their own and the common good. The socializing process can be variously coordinated with individual freedom and development under varying conditions. Temporary necessary interference with the exercise of rights should not extend beyond the emergency. Local, national, and world welfare must be the object of one coordinated or integrated devotion. Christians are by their faith qualified to comply with this requirement. Political views can vary legitimately; education should be such as to lead to mature judgment in civic matters.

In Article 76 the Church distinguishes its role from that of the State or any political community; she is allied to no particular political system. "Wholesome mutual cooperation" of Church and State, mutually independent, is the desideratum. (This sounds a long way from Canossa or the old Papal States!) "For those who dedicate themselves to the ministry of God's Word should use means and helps proper to the gospel. In many respects these differ from the supports of the earthly city." The Church "has the right to pass moral judgments, even on matters touching the political order, whenever basic personal rights or the salvation of souls make such judgments necessary."

Chapter V, the Fostering of Peace and the Promotion of a Community of Nations, consists of an Introduction and two sections. In the Introduction, recognizing that "the whole human family has reached an hour of supreme crisis," the Council calls on each person to devote himself "to the reality of peace" (Art. 77), for, in the words of the gospel, the artisans of peace "shall be called the children of God." Thus the Council goes beyond academic arguments, and calls, beyond the wish for peace, for the will to peace.

"Peace is not merely the absence of war, . . . the maintenance of a balance of power," nor a product of dictatorship: it is " 'an enterprise of justice.' " (Art. 78.) Since the requirements of justice must be fitted to ever-changing conditions, peace is not attained once for all, but must be built up ceaselessly. Since peace requires respect for others, it depends on more than justice, i.e., on brotherhood, the fruit of love. Nonviolence is praised.

(Not as a criticism but as a supplement, we raise the

question whether a useful distinction may not be made here. A tolerable, viable peace based on approximate international justice, and the means for adjusting and maintaining it, should be our peace goal in the first, the contemporary stage. We have in the organization that holds fifty "sovereign states" together in the United States of America, not a model, but an encouraging prototype, for this pragmatic peace. And we have in the World Court and the United Nations at least the prototypes, if not the embryos, of means for preserving justice on a world scale —once we have a reasonably just starting point—and here this chapter is strong. We shall not bring men to desire and create justice without the stimulus and the sacrifice— and the restraint—of love. But, institutionally, the absence of war is a necessity for the development of universal brotherhood. The acceptance of this sequence, first the pragmatic, then the ideal, would help to defeat fatalism, and change the wish to the will.)

Section 1 takes up the avoidance of war. In the face of the increasing horrors of war, obedience to orders cannot excuse those who perpetrate violations of human conscience and universal natural law. Genocide is condemned. International agreements to mitigate the inhumanity of war must be observed and extended and improved. Conscientious objectors—who "refuse to bear arms"— should be allowed to perform "some other form of service to the human community." (Art. 79.)

There is no treatment here of the "just war" doctrine. But the "right to legitimate defense once every means of peaceful settlement has been exhausted" is reaffirmed, as long as "there is no competent and sufficiently powerful authority at the international level." Wars of conquest are denounced. The "mere fact that war has unhappily begun" does not "mean that all is fair between the warring parties." (Art. 79.)

Considering the wholesale destruction wrought by modern weapons, the Council "makes its own the condemnations of total war already pronounced by recent Popes," i.e., Pope John in *Pacem in Terris* and Pope Paul before the United Nations. "Condemnations" is used popularly here, not in the sense usually reserved to anathematize heresy. Speaking more formally, the Council solemnly declared: "Any act of war aimed indiscriminately at the destruction of entire cities or of extensive areas along with their population is a crime against God and man himself." (Art. 80.) It is the rich and "great" powers that are capable of committing this crime, the article concludes. We note that obliteration bombing and fire storms such as that inflicted on Dresden are in the same inhuman and criminal category as atomic holocausts.

In spite of the possible and temporary deterrent effect of armaments, "men should be convinced that the arms race . . . is not a safe way to preserve a steady peace," nor a sure one. The "causes of war threaten" thereby "to grow gradually stronger." Money spent on arms can't be used to remedy the "multiple miseries" of the world. Dependence on armament does not contribute to the real and radical healing of disagreements or remove anxiety. "The arms race is an utterly treacherous trap for humanity, and one which injures the poor to an intolerable degree." (Art. 81.)

The total banning of war "requires the establishment of some universal public authority acknowledged as such by all, and endowed with effective power to safeguard, on the behalf of all, security, regard for justice, and respect for rights." This requires preparation by existing authorities, with reduction of arms by agreement, "not indeed a unilateral disarmament," and the building of mutual trust. Many leaders "work hard to do away with war" (Art. 82); public opinion must support them; education for peace is vital.

Section 2 discusses building up the international community. Among the causes of discord listed are those that "stem from excessive economic inequalities" and slowness in applying remedies, from "a quest for power," and "contempt for personal rights." These "same evils are found in relationships between nations." Hence, "it is altogether necessary that international institutions cooperate to a better and surer extent and that they be coordinated." (Art. 83.) Pope Paul could hardly have endorsed the United Nations more emphatically than he did by leaving the Council to visit it, by speaking to it, and reporting on his visit most impressively to the bishops assembled in Council.

Article 84 underscores the need for various agencies helping to create "an order which corresponds to modern obligations" created by mutual dependence, and by the "intolerable need" of "numerous regions." "The Church rejoices at the spirit of true fraternity flourishing between Christians and non-Christians in all these areas."

Many nations have won their legal independence but have remained unduly dependent economically, requiring both human and financial assistance. Help should be offered "by advanced nations . . . generously and without avarice." "If an economic order is to be created which is genuine and universal, there must be an abolition of excessive desire for profit, nationalistic pretensions, the lust for political domination, militaristic thinking, and intrigues designed to spread and impose ideologies." Then indeed experts might "find common bases for a healthy world trade." (Art. 85.)

Four norms for economic cooperation are proposed in Article 86: a) a self-reliant desire in developing nations for complete human fulfillment; b) recognition and discharge of the obligation of the advanced nations to help the others; c) the international community should coordinate and stimulate economic growth, observing the principle of subsidiarity (higher authorities doing only what lower ones cannot do: this is perhaps not too different from Jefferson's idea of keeping "government" to the minimum); d) reform of economic and social structures where needed, but not hastily or immaturely, not neglecting native traditions or putting material advantages above men's "spiritual nature and development." Again (in "d") we find a theme repeated from the Declaration on the Relationship of the Church to Non-Christian Religions.

"Rapid population growth" is recognized as a problem calling for international cooperation—to improve food production, create a better social order, regulate migration, and to give expert study to the problem. The "Council exhorts all to beware against solutions contradicting the moral law." "The question of how many children should be born belongs to the honest judgment of parents": they must have a "rightly formed conscience," respect the divine law, and take account "of circumstances and the times." Parents should be "judiciously informed of scientific advances" that would aid them in arranging the number of their children: the reliability of such methods and "their harmony with the moral order should be clear." (Art. 87.)

"Christians should collaborate willingly and wholeheartedly in establishing an international order involving genuine respect for all freedoms and amicable brotherhood between all men." It is as though Christ "were crying out" for the poor of the world "to beg the charity of the disciples." Some rich nations count a majority of Christian citizens—who, most of all, should heed this call in "the spirit of poverty." (Art. 88.) Volunteers in relief of poverty deserve praise and support. Ecumenical cooperation is desirable (it is observable at many points, and is supported by the World Council of Churches).

The Church "must be thoroughly present in the midst of the community of nations," through her public institutions and through the full and sincere collaboration of all Christians, "motivated solely by the desire to be of service to all." The "formation of youth in this regard" (Art. 89) requires special care.

Christians have an important obligation and role in forming and participating in agencies of international cooperation. Such agencies should achieve coordination, and a "universal outlook—something certainly appropriate for Catholics" (Art. 90), who are enjoined to cooperate actively and positively "with their separated brothers, who together with them profess the gospel of love, and with all men thirsting for true peace." Article 90 concludes with the proposal to set up "some agency of the universal Church . . . for the world-wide promotion of justice for the poor and of Christ's kind of love for them": that agency is being created. (See *Dialogue #33*, pp. 22-23.)[1]

The Constitution ends with a Conclusion (Arts. 91-93). This program is deliberately general, for all men, in a variety of situations: "We have relied on the Word of God and the spirit of the gospel," hoping "to bring substantial benefit to everyone" (Art. 91) as the program is pursued and amplified.

Dialogue is necessary, and "the Church stands forth as a sign of that brotherliness which allows honest dialogue and invigorates it." The ecumenical spirit is summoned, extending even to attitudes toward "those who oppress the Church and harass her in manifold ways" (Art. 92) (no polemics, no anathemas here). The task requires doing as well as professing, and love as well as aspiration for social betterment: " 'By this will all men know that you are my disciples, if you have love one for another.' " (Art. 93.) Amen!

[1] See footnote 3, p. 59.

## II. AGREEMENTS AND DIFFERENCES

The chief differences among Christians with regard to this Pastoral Constitution on the Church in the Modern World concern the approach to society more than the content of the analysis and proposals, and these differences cut across the three Confessions. Traditionally, the Roman Catholic Church has exerted almost the maximum influence on politics of which it was capable. For six decades in Italy after 1870 this took the form of an attempted boycott. The Eastern Orthodox, while affirming the identity of folk and church, have traditionally emphasized worship rather than "works" in the social milieu. Protestants have been divided in various ways. "Established" churches have tended to be more ruled than ruling; the "free churches," opposed to establishment, are not agreed as to the churches' role in society; the "peace" churches, with a large degree of unanimity, oppose war. Denominations associated in councils become constantly more involved in social action, but their membership is far from unanimous in supporting it—or, indeed, affiliation with the councils—local, state, national, or world.

A most important and rapidly growing *agreement* among Christians of nearly all varieties is that the Christian individual should behave as a Christian citizen. If this tendency continues, it will become increasingly difficult for the member to understand why he should not have the specific and public support and guidance of his church.

An important *difference* between Protestant denominations and the Church of Rome, developed in recent decades, is in the degree of permissiveness for interference with the natural processes of procreation. Only abstinence or the rhythm method are so far normally permitted for Catholics. This difference may be sharpened or blunted when Pope Paul, after considering the report of his reorganized commission, issues new instructions to the faithful. As is evidenced by the Pastoral Constitution, the Catholic Church by no means ignores the world population problem.

Protestants are irked by the position of inferiority assigned to them in mixed marriages. This merits mention here not because of what the Pastoral Constitution says, but because it did not deal with the subject. Pope Paul

made only slight concessions in the directives issued early
in 1966.

Protestants and Orthodox in general must be grateful for
this generally moderate, biblically re-enforced, socially constructive Pastoral Constitution, its ecumenical reminders,
its humane and human orientation. Some may still think
that it diverts the Church from its central task of evangelizing all men; others will see it as a result, a test, a condition
of evangelization.

This Pastoral Constitution is so long and so varied in
content that the student may profit by a few comments
from those who watched its development, from an afterthought as to what to do with a miscellany of agenda re-
mainders, into a Schema XVII, then (as other Schemata
were combined) Schema XIII, and gradually into a major
document, one of the four Constitutions that the Pope and
the Council promulgated.

One thing that stands out is that the need for this
statement is implicit in Pope John's key word, *aggiornamento*—bringing up-to-date, out of the shadows and in-
hibitions of the past, to a recognition of *today's* world
(*"giorno"* means "day") and a sympathetic—not super-
cilious or fearful—entrance into its hazards and its po-
tentialities.

Along with this, partly cause, partly effect, goes a
notable, genuinely revolutionary change of attitude, of
stance, in looking at the world. When Pius IX issued
a century earlier his *Syllabus of Errors* and the more
reasoned encyclicals that it recapitulated, he voiced the
repugnance and apprehension of his Church in face of
a Europe whose politics, economics, science, and philosophy increasingly ignored or opposed religion. His reaction
may have been all that Catholicism in his day was prepared for. Succeeding Popes did much to encourage workingmen. Theologians and other churchmen began to sense
the ecumenical imperative. And before they knew it themselves, Catholics were ready to begin, at least, to understand and love the world. One may hazard the prediction
that this change of stance, this effort, will have more effect
on the world's culture than the praiseworthy but somewhat pedestrian section of the Constitution devoted to that
subject.

The Dogmatic Constitution on the Church is the foundation, the warrant, the reservoir, the sine qua non, for

the total output of Vatican II. But it gradually became clear to the bishops and their expert aides that it was not enough to say what the Church is: one must know what it is for, what it is to do; one vision without the other is incomplete, blurred.

The Pastoral Constitution completes the Dogmatic Constitution in general and in various particulars. It helps to give direction and content to the Decree on Ecumenism and to statements, in various places, on the laity. And it lays some of the foundations for building world peace.

We turn first to world peace. If religion, with the increased leverage of the growing and widening and maturing ecumenical movement, does not vastly augment and re-enforce the will to peace and inspire a concerted and unremitting attack on the causes of war, the hope for peace is indeed a faint one—and the outlook for religion not brilliant.

The Council's leads are valuable. While it did not issue a resounding denunciation of war as sin, it justified defensive war, not on the basis of the "just war" doctrine, but on the absence, the lack, of any world authority at present capable of enforcing peace. It also called for an international attack on poverty, with something more constructive than doles, and provided for Vatican machinery to help coordinate the war on poverty and constructive efforts for peace. There has been much useful cooperation and coordination of action between Catholic and Protestant agencies in relief and refugee work. The stage is now set for more than salvage operations: famines must be prevented, poverty abolished. The possibility can now be confidently affirmed. The techniques are known; the material resources are in sight. Inertia and greed are the obstacles. Given the population pressure, of whose gravity the Council took note, and the limited and precarious character of the peace that the world now has, which the Council emphasized, the time available for effective peace action may be tragically short. In this situation, inertia is both sinful and stupid. And greed, on the part of a nation, is not only sinful, as the Council indicated; it is incredibly short-sighted and self-defeating.

The ecumenical movement is challenged by the Pastoral Constitution on the Church in the Modern World not only for the struggle against war and poverty, but for united effort in education, the elevation of culture and morality, the overcoming of racial, national, class, and religious prejudices, and indeed the nurture of faith itself. The Church-in-the-world is doomed to frustration on other than a wide and expanding ecumenical base; the ecumenical movement would be deprived of at least half its potentiality, unless it takes the churches into those troubled areas "where cross the crowded ways of life."

Much of the above will disturb many devoted Christians until they take due cognizance of the tremendous responsibility that it throws upon laymen. According to the Pastoral Constitution, laymen are not only to hold up the hands of the clergy, to support the Church: they are, practically, the Church *in the world*. This may well prove to be the greatest significance of the Pastoral Constitution. It enlists the Church, officially and essentially (hence a "Constitution"), in the unremitting and undefeatable campaign for a morally constituted, morally functioning social order, and calls laymen, as the major portion of the universal priesthood of believers, to a strategic and vital position, front and center, in the struggle, with God's help, to make the City of Man more like the City of God.

## III. QUESTIONS FOR DISCUSSION

1. Why is this Pastoral Constitution on the Church in the Modern World so important to ecumenical relations?

2. What is its attitude in regard to world peace?

3. How far does it go in supporting birth control?

4. To what degree does this Constitution give a basis for practical ecumenical action?

5. What should be the relationship of the Church to secular society?

6. How are the religious faiths already cooperating in the areas of peace-making, world relief, and race relations?

7. Why is it so important to preserve the human values in modern society?

8. How can the Church become the Servant of Mankind?

## IV. SUGGESTIONS FOR ECUMENICAL ACTION

1. Read the Pastoral Constitution on the Church in the

Modern World as found in *The Documents of Vatican II*.

2. Attend a session of the United Nations.

3. Participate in some project which is supporting some great cause in a practical way.

4. Compare the statements of the World Council of Churches with those of the Second Vatican Council in regard to the Church in the modern world.

5. Note how the Vatican and the World Council of Churches are working together to implement the views expressed in this Constitution and in the WCC Conference on the Church and Society (1966).

"Wishing to intensify the apostolic activity of the People of God, this most holy Synod earnestly addresses itself to the laity, whose proper and indispensable role in the mission of the Church it has already called to mind in other documents. The layman's apostolate derives from his Christian vocation, and the Church can never be without it. Sacred Scripture clearly shows how spontaneous and fruitful such activity was at the very beginning of the Church (cf. Acts 11:19-21; 18:26; Rom. 16:1-16; Phil. 4:3)." (From the Introduction to the Decree on the Apostolate of the Laity.)

# CHAPTER VI

# The Role of the Laity

## INTRODUCTION

The reform and renewal movement within the Roman Catholic Church is reflected in a significant manner in the Decree on the Apostolate of the Laity (*Apostolicam Actuositatem*) which was promulgated by Pope Paul VI on November 18, 1965. Here it is stressed that the ministry of the Church (the People of God) is one and that the laity are a real part of this ministry which has two principal parts: 1) the ministry of the individual by holy living and by example, and 2) the influence of the lay person in the affairs of the world.

## I. THE POSITION OF THE DECREE

As in several other documents of the Second Vatican Council, this Decree declared that the laity constitute "the

People of God" and these People of God constitute the visible Church. Because the laity are a major part of the Church "the layman's apostolate derives from his Christian vocation and the Church can never be without it." (Art. 1.) Scripture and the life of the early Church confirm this position.

Because of this divine origin and because modern conditions demand even greater zeal on the part of the laity, the Introduction indicates the sacred mandate given to the laity: "Our own times require of the laity no less zeal. In fact, modern conditions demand that their apostolate be thoroughly broadened and intensified. The constant expansion of population, scientific and technical progress, and the tightening of bonds between men have not only immensely widened the field of the lay apostolate, a field which is for the most part accessible only to them." (Art. 1.)

It is pointed out in Chapter I that the Church was founded for the purpose of spreading the Kingdom of Christ throughout the entire world and that all Christians have a sacred obligation to participate in this task. While there are different ministries in the Church—bishops, priests, teachers, etc.—there is only one ministry and the People of God are directly related to it. Their ministry is not a passive one, but one of action. In fact, "the member who fails to make his proper contribution to the development of the Church must be said to be useful neither to the Church nor to himself." (Art. 2.)

This ministry of the laity has a twofold character: "They exercise a genuine apostolate in fact by their activity directed on behalf of bringing the gospel and holiness to men and on behalf of penetrating and perfecting the temporal sphere of things through the spirit of the gospel." (Art. 2.) Those who engage in this two-fold ministry are aided by special gifts from the Holy Spirit.

Chapter II deals with the goals to be achieved. Here again is stressed the fact that "the mission of the Church is not only to bring to men the message and grace of Christ, but also to penetrate and perfect the temporal sphere with the spirit of the gospel." (Art. 5.) Therefore there is this dual objective, not only to bring the saving grace of Christ to other individuals but also to renew and constantly perfect the modern world. The latter is a "special obligation" of the laity.

Participation in social welfare is therefore essential to the lay Christian. "Wherever there are people in need of food and drink, clothing, housing, medicine, employment, education; wherever men lack the facilities necessary for living a truly human life or are tormented by hardships or poor health, or suffer exile or imprisonment, there Christian charity should seek them out and find them, console them with eager care and relieve them with the gift of help." (Art. 8.)

Christian charity, however, must be accompanied by social justice. It is not enough merely to remedy personal ills; their *causes* also must be rooted out. "Not only the effects but also the causes of various ills must be removed. Help should be given in such a way that the recipients may gradually be freed from dependence on others and become self-sufficient." (Art. 8.)

Chapter Three of the Decree deals with the various fields of the apostolate of the laity: 1) within the Church itself, 2) within the immediate community, 3) within the family, 4) on the part of youth, 5) in public affairs, and 6) in the international situation. Here the decree points out that the People of God must be Christians in all their relations within the institutional Church itself and then reach out into the community in Christian service. It also stresses the point that "the apostolate of married persons and of families is of unique importance for the Church and civil society." (Art. 11.)

Special attention in the Decree is given to youth. It points out that young persons exert a very important influence in modern society. "There has been a complete change in the circumstances of their lives, their mental attitudes, and their relationship with their own families. Frequently they move too quickly into new social and economic conditions. While their social and even their political importance is growing from day to day, they seem to be unable to cope adequately with the new burdens imposed upon them." (Art. 12.)

Therefore, says the Decree, adults ought to engage in such friendly discussions with young people that both age groups, overcoming the age barrier, will become better acquainted with each other and share the special benefits each generation can offer. Youth's zest for life should be dedicated to the service of Christ.

"As they become more conscious of their own personality, they are impelled by a zest for life and abounding energies to assume their own responsibility, and they yearn to play their part in social and cultural life. If this zeal is imbued with the spirit of Christ and is inspired by obedience to and love for the shepherds of the Church, it can be expected to be very fruitful. They themselves ought to become the prime and direct apostles of youth, exercising the apostolate among themselves and through themselves and reckoning with the social environment in which they live." (Art. 12.)

The ecumenical spirit is indicated when Catholics here are instructed to cooperate with all men and women of good will to promote whatever is true, whatever just, whatever holy, whatever lovable. They are encouraged to take an active part in civic affairs in order to help promote the common good and to take a direct interest in foreign affairs, "especially with respect to developing nations." (Art. 14.) And those who travel abroad, whether their interest is international affairs, business, or pleasure are reminded that they are itinerant heralds of Christ wherever they go and should act accordingly.

In the fourth chapter instructions are given about the various forms of the apostolate: personal, through small groups, or through national and international associations.

Chapter Five makes the point that all the lay apostolate is to be under the direction of the hierarchy of the Church. It says specifically that no project can claim the name "Catholic" unless it has obtained the consent of the lawful Church authority. While it is true that the laity is entrusted with certain functions such as the teaching of Christian doctrine, certain liturgical actions, and the care of souls, nevertheless, by virtue of this mission "the laity are fully subject to higher ecclesiastical direction in the performance of such work." Furthermore, the hierarchy has the "right to judge"—after careful consideration of all related matters and consultation with experts—"whether or not such activities and institutions conform to moral principles. It also has the right to decide what is required for the protection and promotion of values of the supernatural order." (Art. 24.) Bishops, pastors of parishes, and other priests are asked to keep in mind that the laity, while under the control of the hierarchy, have their own role in building up the Church. They are urged to cooperate just as much as possible in the lay apostolic mission by seeing that the laity gets proper spiritual aid and instruction.

The last chapter deals with the kind of training needed for the lay apostolate.

> "Since laymen share in their own way in the mission of the Church, their apostolic formation takes its special flavor from the distinctively secular quality of the lay state and from its own form of spirituality. . . .
>
> "Formation for the apostolate means a certain human and well-rounded formation adapted to the natural abilities and circumstances of each lay person. Well-informed about the modern world, the lay person should be an active member of his own society and be adjusted to its culture. . . .
>
> "However, the lay person should learn to advance the mission of Christ and the Church by basing his life on belief in the divine mystery of creation and redemption, and by being sensitive to the movement of the Holy Spirit, who gives life to the People of God and who would impel all men to love God the Father as well as the world and mankind in Him. This formation should be deemed the basis and condition for every successful apostolate." (Ch. VI, Art. 29.)

Each person is also encouraged to get a solid doctrinal instruction in theology, ethics, and philosophy—adjusted of course to differences of age, status, and natural talents. Moreover, this training should be a life-time experience, whether in the family or through advanced education in schools and colleges.

## II. THE LAITY AND PROTESTANTISM

It is essential that the new Catholic position in regard to the laity, as reflected officially in the documents of Vatican II, be examined in relation to the reports on the laity made at the Third Assembly of the World Council of Churches held at New Delhi, India, in 1961 (a year before the opening of the Council). It is interesting to note how this conference of Protestant and Orthodox church leaders, in some respects, paved the way for "advanced" positions at the Second Vatican Council. It should also be noted—and this is a fundamental difference—that the Council had as official delegates only members of the hierarchy (bishops of the Church), while the New Delhi Assembly had, on an equal basis, clergy and laity and, moreover, both men and women.

The report of the Committee for the Department of the Laity of the World Council of Churches at New Delhi wrestled with the definition of the laity in this manner:

> "Some say that laymen are those Christians who are not ordained; others maintain that baptism is an ordination and that all Christians are therefore ordained for a ministry. Some say that laymen are those who gain their livelihood in a secular occupation; others point to the many church-employed professional 'laymen' and to the specially ordained voluntary clergy. Some say that laymen are those who have not studied theology; others claim that Christians involved fulltime in politics, education, etc., need theological discernment no less than pastors or other professional church workers. While acknowledging the fact that there is still no ecumenical consensus about the term laity, most of the committee members emphasized the wholeness of the *laos,* the laity. Wherever in this report and elsewhere any of the above-mentioned distinctions within the *laos* must be made in order to show the complementary character of different relationships within Christ's Body, these must never be considered as divisions but as the development of the varied gifts and ministries within the total ministry of Christ."

The report goes on to emphasize the fact that Christian laymen have the obligation to serve as the channel of Christ's light to the whole world, and that a sharp distinction between the "religious" and the "secular" does not exist. It makes the point that all of creation is God's; all of it is the theater of his judgment, mercy, and glory.

Prior to the Second Vatican Council, the New Delhi Assembly noted that all members of the Church, "the People of God," are called to follow Christ and act as

His witnesses in the world. Christian service is the keynote. Worship and service in everyday life are closely related. "Laymen must provide a two-way channel of communications between Church and world."

It is significant that at the Fourth World Conference on Faith and Order of the World Council of Churches, at Montreal, Canada, in 1963, special stress was placed upon the total ministry of the People of God (which was later also stressed by the Second Vatican Council). It declared that "a recovery of a true doctrine of the laity has brought with it the recognition that ministry is the responsibility of the whole body and not only of those who are ordained. This discovery is one of the most important facts of recent church history."

It is also significant that at the Montreal Conference stress was placed upon "a special ministry" in which laymen might serve.

Although most of the denominations believe that ordination is a special calling of the Lord, and has separate standing and responsibilities, they do not (with perhaps the exception of "high church" Episcopalians) believe that they are given additional graces or powers not in the possession of the dedicated layman. Therefore in Protestant churches are found laymen who serve on official boards of the church, are moderators of local congregations, and are lay preachers. Some laymen give a few years of their lives to special missionary services. Others serve as Christian teachers, both on a voluntary and on a professional basis. Many laymen are Y.M.C.A. and Y.W.C.A. secretaries and serve in other "secular" areas of service in the community. A few laymen become heads of national denominational bodies.

Protestants also have their "religious": those non-ordained Christians who have given themselves completely, on a full-time basis, to Christian service. The great difference between Protestants and Catholics is that the latter have a hierarchy (bishops along with the Pope) which rules the Church authoritatively and largely without the benefit of the laity.

The Eastern Orthodox Church in most respects seems to be much closer to Roman Catholicism than to Protestantism. In the area of ecclesiastical government and practice the situation is different. Orthodox churches take pride in their democratic system of church government. They have long encouraged their laity to read and pattern their lives on the Bible and to stress spiritual experience through divine worship rather than ecclesiastical authority.

Both in Protestantism and in the Eastern Orthodox churches the laity (even taking into consideration the stress on the People of God and the special ministry of the laity as advanced by the Second Vatican Council) are in a much stronger position than they are in the Roman Catholic Church. This is clearly manifest not only in the administrative functions of the Church, but also in the ministry and in the ecclesiastical control of higher education and parochial schools in general. While the Catholic layman is causing much excitement in such areas as academic freedom and birth control, it can be fairly stated that he is still on the way to freedom and has not yet achieved it. Compared with non-Catholics he still has a long way to go.

Protestant and Orthodox leaders have been conscious of the role of the laity in the Church for many decades. For example, at the founding of the World Council of Churches in Amsterdam in 1948 it was noted that "this is the day of opportunity for the lay membership of the Church." Then, like Vatican II, it declared that

> "the work of God requires that every member of the Church, ordained and lay, be an active witness. The layman has his duties in the Church in worship and stewardship. He is charged also with a task in the world outside. The most obvious sphere of witness is the home, the place in which the Church of the coming generation is to be built up. Some are called to special ministries of preaching and intercession. For most people the field of witness lies in the place where they do their daily work. The way in which they do their job or exercise their profession must be unmistakably Christian. . . . Christian service *is* to be conceived in the widest possible terms. The variety of forms of witness is just the means by which God can make known the fulness of the gospel as His answer to the needs of mankind."

While Vatican II encouraged the laity to take similar action, the laity (both men and women) are greatly restricted in the exercise of authority and action within the Roman Catholic Church. At Vatican II no layman had any official part in the Council. The documents on the laity and communications suffered because laymen were not a part of the commission which composed these decrees. Even after Vatican II, unlike both Protestant and Orthodox sections of the Church, the laymen of the Roman Catholic Church are still under strict ecclesiastical control and even their own organizations have to have clearance in all important matters from the bishop of the diocese. Such restrictions are indicative of the vast difference which exists between Protestant and Orthodox churches and the Roman Catholic Church in regard to the nature of the Church. While new emphasis is being placed upon the whole People of God, the Roman Catholic Church has not yet given the layman any degree of real authority in the policy-making and government of the Church. Protestants and Orthodox are waiting for it to catch up at this essential point, as it has done in such areas as religious liberty, biblical research, and ecumenical relations.

The First Assembly of the World Council of Churches, Amsterdam, Holland, 1948, had this to say concerning the laity:

> "The laity constitutes more than 99% of the Church.
>
> "In the customary work of the Church (preaching, evangelizing, teaching, and social work) the latent spiritual resources of the rank and file are urgently needed. It is commonly assumed that this need is widely and sufficiently recognized, but in fact it is not.
>
> "There is, however, another aspect of this problem of the laity of even greater import for the Church in its relation to the world. Laymen and women spend the greater part of their lives in their homes, their occupations, and the public life of the community. It is essential that the churches should take note of this. For it is through the laity that the Church has the greatest and most natural opportunity to show in and to the world that the message of the Bible, and all that the Church is committed to by obedience to its Lord, are relevant to the real problems and needs of man in every age, and not least in our own. Only by the witness of a spiritually intelligent and active laity can the Church meet the modern world in its actual

perplexities and life situations. Since one of the hard facts of the present time is that millions of people think of the Church as floating above the modern world and entirely out of real touch with it, the importance of this simple pronouncement cannot easily be overestimated."

In the Report of Section VI on "The Laity—The Christian in His Vocation," received by the second assembly of the World Council of Churches, Evanston, Illinois, 1954, it is stated:

"Clergy and laity belong together in the Church; if the Church is to perform her mission in the world, they need each other. The growing emphasis in many parts of the world upon the function of the laity since the Amsterdam Assembly is not to be understood as an attempt to secure for the laity some larger place of recognition in the Church, nor yet as merely a means to supplement an overburdened and understaffed ordained ministry. It springs from the rediscovery of the true nature of the Church as the People of God. The word 'laity' must not be understood in a merely negative way as meaning those church members who are not clergy. Though not yet fully articulated, a more positive understanding of the ministry of the laity is gaining acceptance. The phrase 'the ministry of the laity' expresses the privilege of the whole Church to share in Christ's ministry to the world. We must understand anew the implications of the fact that we are all baptized into Christ and that as Christ came to minister so must all Christians become ministers of His saving purpose according to the particular gift of the Spirit which each has received, as messengers of the hope revealed in Christ. Therefore in daily living and work the laity are not mere fragments of the Church who are scattered about in the world and who come together again for worship, instruction, and specifically Christian fellowship on Sundays. They are the Church's representatives, no matter where they are. It is the laity who draw together work and worship; it is they who bridge the gulf between the Church and the world, and it is they who manifest in word and action the Lordship of Christ over that world which claims so much of their time and energy and labor. This, and not some new order or organization, is the ministry of the laity. They are called to it because they belong to the Church, although many do not yet know that they are thus called."

## III. QUESTIONS FOR DISCUSSION

1. What new advantages are given Catholic laymen through the Decree on the Apostolate of the Laity adopted by Vatican Council II?

2. What is the basic difference between the laity in the Roman Catholic Church and non-Catholic churches?

3. How can Catholic and Protestant laymen join in preaching the gospel?

4. Why is there trouble in Catholic colleges concerning academic freedom?

5. At what points do Catholic and non-Catholic laymen see eye to eye?

6. Why were Catholic laymen not permitted to participate officially in the Second Vatican Council?

7. What was the difference between Catholic "auditors" and Protestant "observers" at the Council?

8. What is meant by the term "People of God"?

9. Are laymen more inclined toward ecumenical action than the clergy?

## IV. SUGGESTIONS FOR ECUMENICAL ACTION

1. Read the full Decree on the Apostolate of the Laity in *The Documents of Vatican II.*

2. Discuss with a layman of another faith how the Second Vatican Council has made a difference in his status within the Church.

3. Discover why there are so many student and faculty strikes in Catholic and Protestant colleges and universities.

4. Visit a parochial school (Catholic or Protestant) to find out how it is staffed, controlled, and financed.

5. Discover how you can promote Christian principles within your own vocation.

6. Join an interfaith group in the study of *Living Room Dialogues.* (See Bibliography at the end of this book.)

"The present historical situation is leading humanity into a new stage. As the salt of the earth and light of the world (cf. Mt. 5:13-14), the Church is summoned with special urgency to save and renew every creature. In this way all things can be restored in Christ, and in Him mankind can compose one family and one people." (Preface, Decree on the Missionary Activity of the Church.)

CHAPTER VII

# The Christian Missionary Witness

## INTRODUCTION

Three chief emphases are made in the Decree on the Missionary Activity of the Church: 1) that the "pilgrim Church" is missionary by its very nature; 2) that, insofar as religious conditions will allow, the mission of the Church should be conducted within the ecumenical spirit. (The former is Biblical; the latter is one of the new Christian contributions of the Second Vatican Council.)

The third emphasis, which is relatively new, is that laymen should cooperate actively in the missionary task of the Church and they should "gladly offer socio-economic cooperation to the peoples on the way to development." (Art. 41.)

This Decree (Ad Gentes) was promulgated by Pope Paul VI on December 7, 1965.

## I. THE ROMAN CATHOLIC CHURCH IN MISSION

Chapter I begins with the statement that "the pilgrim Church is missionary by her very nature." (Art. 2.) It is from the mission of Christ and the mission of the Holy Spirit that she draws her origin. And the universal design of God for the salvation of the human race is revealed by Scripture. Moreover, the Church Fathers have proclaimed that whatever has not been taken up by Christ, and fulfilled in Him, is not made whole.

> "The mission of the Church, therefore, is fulfilled by that activity which makes her fully present to all men and nations. She undertakes this activity in obedience to Christ's command and in response to the grace and love of the Holy Spirit. Thus, by the example of her life and by her preaching, by the sacraments and other means of grace, she can lead them to the faith, the freedom, and the peace of Christ. Thus there lies open before them a free and trustworthy road to full participation in the mystery of Christ." (Ch. I, Art. 5.)

In carrying out this divine mission the gospel must be preached to all, and especially to the poor, and the Church herself "must walk the same road which Christ walked: a road of poverty and obedience, of service and self-sacrifice to the death, from which death He came forth a victor by His resurrection." (Art. 5.)

Therefore, the term "missions" is given to those heralds of the gospel who are sent out into all the world by the Church to carry out the task of preaching and living the gospel and planting the Church among peoples or groups who do not believe in Christ. "Therefore, all must be converted to Him as He is made known by the Church's preaching. All must be incorporated into Him by baptism, and into the Church which is His body." (Art. 7.)

Although God, in ways known only to Himself, may lead those "inculpably ignorant" of the gospel to find that faith without which it is impossible to please Him, nevertheless the Church of necessity, as a sacred duty, must preach the gospel to all people everywhere. And the members of the Church are impelled to carry on missionary activity by reason of the love "with which they love God and by which they desire to share with all men in the spiritual goods of both this life and the life to come." (Art. 7.)

". . . By himself and by his own power, no one is freed from sin or raised above himself, or completely rid of his sickness or his solitude or his servitude. On the contrary, all stand in need of Christ, their Model, their Mentor, their Liberator, their Savior, their Source of life.

"The gospel has truly been a leaven of liberty and progress in human history, even in its temporal sphere, and always proves itself a leaven of brotherhood, of unity, and of peace." (Art. 8.)

It is pointed out in Chapter II, on mission work itself, that the Church is fully aware that there still remains "a gigantic missionary task for her to accomplish." (Art. 10.) The gospel message has not yet, or hardly yet, been heard by two billion human beings. Moreover, their number is increasing daily. Some of these people are followers of the great non-Christian religions; others remain strangers to the very knowledge of God; while still others expressly deny His existence and sometimes oppose it.

In order to win such people to the gospel of Christ the Church must implant herself in their very midst and bear living testimony to the saving power of Christ. And thus Christian charity and witness extends "to all, without distinction of race, social condition, or religion." (Art. 12.)

Stress is placed upon the education of children and youth, upon public service, and especially in the developing nations upon the striving toward the full uplifting of human dignity and better living conditions. "Furthermore, let the faithful take part in the strivings of those peoples who are waging war on famine, ignorance, and disease and thereby struggling to better their way of life and to secure peace in the world. In this activity, the faithful should be eager to offer their prudent aid to projects sponsored by public and private organizations, by governments, by international agencies, by various Christian communities, and even by non-Christian religions." (Art. 12.)

It is emphasized in the Decree that "the Church in no way desires to inject herself into the government of the earthly city." Moreover, "The Church strictly forbids forcing anyone to embrace the faith, or alluring or enticing people by unworthy techniques. By the same token, she also strongly insists on a person's right not to be deterred from the faith by unjust vexations on the part of others." (Art. 13.) It is stated that, according to the Church's ancient custom, the convert's motives should be looked into and if necessary purified.

A section of Chapter II (Arts. 15–18) is given over

to forming the Christian community, indicating that it should always be kept in mind that the local church is a real and full part of the Church Universal.

In the building of the Christian community special stress is placed upon ecumenical relationships.

> "The ecumenical spirit too should be nurtured in the neophytes. They should rightly consider that the brethren who believe in Christ are Christ's disciples, reborn in baptism, sharers with the People of God in very many riches. Insofar as religious conditions allow, ecumenical activity should be furthered in such a way that without any appearance of indifference or of unwarranted intermingling on the one hand, or of unhealthy rivalry on the other, Catholics can cooperate in a brotherly spirit with their separated brethren, according to the norms of the Decree on Ecumenism.
>
> "To the extent that their beliefs are common, they can make before the nations a common profession of faith in God and in Jesus Christ. They can collaborate in social and in technical projects as well as in cultural and religious ones." (Art. 15.)

Racial prejudice and hypernationalism should be avoided, the Decree states. Special attention must be given to the Christian laity "who have been incorporated into Christ by baptism and who live in the world." (Art. 15.) Requirements of priestly training, in relation to missionary service, should be combined with an attempt to make contact with the people whom they serve. They should do this with an open mind, with appreciation for the nation's culture. When priests are not available, then deacons should be trained to render a similar service (and they, under certain circumstances, should be allowed to marry). "Let missionaries learn the languages to the extent of being able to use them in a fluent and polished manner. Thus they will find more easy access to the minds and hearts of men. Furthermore, they should be properly introduced into special pastoral problems." (Ch. IV, Art. 26.)

Attention is given to the proper use of mass communication, to the building of churches, and to training institutes.

Authority for missionary activity is placed under one office, namely the office of the Propagation of the Faith.

It issues the directives and develops the programs. It coordinates mission work throughout the world.

> "In the direction of this office, an active role with a deliberative vote should be exercised by selected representatives of all those who cooperate in missionary work. The latter include the bishops of the whole world (whose Episcopal Conferences will have to be heard from in this matter), as well as the moderators of papal institutes and activities whose representatives will be chosen in ways and under conditions to be determined by the Roman Pontiff. All these representatives will be called together at fixed times and will exercise supreme control of all mission work, under the authority of the Supreme Pontiff." (Ch. V, Art. 29.)

In Chapter VI under the topic Missionary Cooperation, it is indicated that since the whole Church is missionary, and the work of evangelization is a basic duty of the People of God, the Council "invites all to a deep interior renewal." (Art. 35.) It emphasizes the point that a profoundly Christian life is basic to all missionary work. This applies not only to the laity but also to priests and bishops. Laymen with special training are called to cooperate with other Christians, and with non-Christians, that their lives may be a witness to Christ.

In conclusion (Art. 42) the Decree ends with these words:

> "The Council Fathers together with the Roman Pontiff, aware of their most solemn duty to spread everywhere the Kingdom of God, lovingly salute all heralds of the gospel. They especially salute those who suffer persecution for the name of Christ, and they make themselves companions in their sufferings.
>
> "These Fathers and the Roman Pontiff are afire with that same love with which Christ burned toward men. But knowing that it is God who makes His Kingdom come on earth, they pour forth their prayers together with all the Christian faithful, that through the intercession of the Virgin Mary, Queen of the Apostles, the nations may be led to the knowledge of the truth as soon as possible (1 Tim. 2:4) and that

the splendor of God which brightens the face of Jesus Christ may shine upon all men through the Holy Spirit" (2 Cor. 4:6).

## II. THE PROTESTANT AND ORTHODOX POSITION

At New Delhi in 1961 the missionary and the ecumenical concerns were united through the integration of the International Missionary Council into the World Council of Churches. It marked a new stage in the Christian world mission. At that moment the old distinction between "sending" and "receiving" churches was broken down. Now all churches are partners in mission, on a plane of mutuality; in the mission of making Christ known, loved, and obeyed throughout the world. Now in the World Council of Churches there is the Division of World Mission and Evangelism.

The Protestant and Orthodox position in regard to mission and evangelism can be stated in these words of the introduction to the report on *Witness* at New Delhi:

"We live in critical times, but it is not because of the desperate nature of the problems of our age that the task of witness to the gospel of Christ is urgent today. The urgency of the Church's evangelistic task arises from the gospel itself, because it is the gospel of Jesus Christ. Christ loves the world, which He died to save. He is already the light of the world, of which He is Lord, and His light has preceded the bearers of the good news into the darkest places. The task of Christian witness is to point to Him as the true light, which is already shining. In Christ was life, and the life was the light of men, the light that enlightens every man. The work of evangelism is necessary in this and in every age in order that the blind eyes may be opened to the splendor of light."

Up to this point the Roman Catholic and the non-Roman Catholic churches have much in common. They both see the need, in a revolutionary world, of helping people and nations solve their problems of living together. They both realize that it is either a matter of peace or perish. They both know that there is a battle on today to save man, and humanity, from moral and spiritual and physical ruin.

New world situations demand of the churches not only a new strategy but also a new sense of unity. And this includes the Roman Catholic Church. Already the World Council of Churches is working with the Vatican in the area of fighting poverty and starvation in various parts of the world.

When it comes to the matter of conversion or proselytization, the Eastern Orthodox churches have no desire to be drawn into the picture, because this is not a part of their ecclesiastical practice. Although there is now a much greater degree of cooperation between the Roman Catholic Church and Protestants, the issue of converts still exists —abroad as at home. And it will continue to exist as long as the two branches of Christendom have different views concerning the saving nature of the Church and the issue of the "one true Church."

The hope of the Christian world mission, as far as the total Christian enterprise is concerned, is found in these words from the Montreal Conference on Faith and Order:

> "If the unity which is 'God's will and His gift to His Church' is to be made visible, it is essential that local churches accept the missionary obligation which God has given to His whole Church. More insistently and urgently than for centuries, we are being asked: 'Are you really sharing the life that is in Jesus Christ, because to share in it is to take part in His mission to the world?'
>
> "It is only as all in each place respond to this call to be God's people in and for their particular 'world,' as well as in and for the whole world, that they will enter into the unity of one committed fellowship."

Professor A. C. Outler made the remark, in connection with the theological conference at Notre Dame (1966) relating to the documents of Vatican II, that the Decree on the Missionary Activity of the Church might well be considered a "sleeper." Apparently what he meant by this was that it had great possibilities which would be realized sometime in the immediate future; that in the document were germ-statements and propositions which, although potent, would take some time to develop. This is probably true, especially when related to the new position on Christian mission which was achieved at the New Delhi Assembly in 1961 of the World Council of Churches.

At New Delhi the Protestant and Orthodox churches not only integrated the International Missionary Council and the World Council of Churches to form a new Division of World Mission and Evangelism, but also faced into a new missionary situation which called for active cooperation and a new strategy. It recognized the fact that in the new world situation missionary responsibility cannot be separated from any other aspect of the Church's life and teaching.

In a statement similar to the one found in the Vatican document it said:

> "The Christian mission is one throughout the world, for there is but one gospel of salvation for all men, one Savior and Lord, who is the light of the world. Today, thanks to the faithful witness of those who went before us in the missionary movement, the Christian mission has a world-wide base. Every Christian congregation is part of that mission, with a responsibility to bear witness to Christ in its own neighborhood and to share in the bearing of that witness to the ends of the earth."

Like the Second Vatican Council the New Delhi Assembly indicated that the new world situation demanded an ecumenical approach. As it took the missionary movement to its very heart in spirit and in program it urged the missionary agencies of the various denominations to place their own work in an ecumenical perspective and accept whatever new insights God might give through new relationships.

Also like the Second Vatican Council, the New Delhi Assembly in 1961 declared that the missionary task is far from being finished. "It is rather entering upon a new and more challenging phase. All our concerns for one another must not cause us to forget the fact that two-thirds of the human race are without the knowledge of Christ as light of the world. We owe them that knowledge. We have no better claim to Christ than they have. Nothing else that we can offer them is a discharge of that debt."

The World Council of Churches at New Delhi pointed

out that the calling of God to His Church today is for a new offering of life itself. For many young people this will mean a life of missionary service abroad. But more than that—for all of every age, of every church, of every nation, it is a call to total and unconditional commitment to the mission of God. It also called for a careful survey of needs in various parts of the world, a redeployment of missionary funds, personnel, and material, and much more joint action.

In working out new relationships it indicated a close co-operation with the Division of Inter-Church Aid and Service to Refugees, with the Division of Studies, with the Division of Ecumenical Action, and with National Christian Councils in Asia, Africa, and Latin America and the Churches of the West.

While there may be differences in regard to hierarchy and doctrine, it is quite remarkable how close Vatican II and New Delhi were brought together largely because of the new world situation. Although New Delhi did not stress as much as Vatican II the matter of cooperating with those of another faith, the fact that it had several Roman Catholic observers present (for the first time) spoke louder than words.

Dr. Eugene L. Smith, Executive Secretary of the American section of the World Council of Churches, in writing a Response to the Decree on the Missionary Activity of the Church in *The Documents of Vatican II* (p. 631) indicates several shortcomings of the document, from the Protestant viewpoint, and raises several questions. He points out that although the missionary call of laity in mission is rightly stressed, nevertheless the participation is to be channeled by the hierarchy. He says, "Fulfillment of the missionary obligation which the Christian discovers in Christ demands opportunity for individual, creative initiative and experimentation which the hierarchical controls assumed in this document would seem severely to restrict."

Dr. Smith also finds fault with the Decree's treatment of missions as primarily "foreign missions" and of missionaries as primarily evangelists sent *abroad*. He is also troubled by the complexity of the organizational problems within the Roman Catholic missionary enterprise which overshadow the vast complexity of the missionary task today.

## III. QUESTIONS FOR DISCUSSION

1. Since "the Church on earth is missionary in its very nature," and "the faithful gathered in the parish church taking part in the Eucharistic liturgy are the Church of God" (according to Father Gregory Baum), what is the missionary function of the local congregation?

2. What is the relationship between missions and the struggle for justice in society?

3. What is the relationship between Christian faith and other religions?

4. What are the conditions under which cooperation can occur in missionary activity between Roman Catholics and other Christians?

5. What is the role of the Holy Spirit today in Christian mission? Do we understand that role primarily as acting through the institutions of the Church, as seemingly implied in the Decree?

6. What future forms of institutional witness should we anticipate in the Christian mission?

## IV. SUGGESTIONS FOR ECUMENICAL ACTION

1. Study the Decree on the Missionary Activity of the Church as found in *The Documents of Vatican II*.

2. Secure a Catholic (or Protestant) missionary magazine and find out whether its editorials and articles are "in tune" with the Decree.

3. Write an official of your local diocese or the American office of the World Council of Churches (475 Riverside Drive, New York City 10027) to discover what missionary tasks Roman Catholics and non-Catholics are doing together.

4. Discover why both Catholic and Protestant missionaries have been forced to leave certain areas in the Far East.

5. Actively support some missionary cause through your denomination.

6. Help some "secular" missionary project.

# PART THREE

# Implementation:
# In Christian Education
# and Mass Communications

"The Decree [on the Instruments of Social Communication] does mark the first time that a general Council of the Church addressed itself to the problem of communication. It is important for this more than for its content. The Decree also marks the first general mandate of the Church to the clergy and laity on the use of communications media."
—Thomas J. M. Burke, S.J., in *The Documents of Vatican II*. (P. 317.)

"Since every man of whatever race, condition, and age is endowed with the dignity of a person, he has an inalienable right to an education corresponding to his proper destiny and suited to his native talents, his sex, his cultural background, and his ancestral heritage. At the same time, this education should pave the way to brotherly association with other peoples, so that genuine unity and peace on earth may be promoted." (From Art. 1 of the Declaration on Christian Education.)

## CHAPTER VIII

# Christian Education, Priestly Training, and Ministry

## INTRODUCTION

Since the whole area of Christian education includes the training and ministry of priests three documents are grouped together in this chapter: the Declaration on Christian Education, the Decree on Priestly Formation, and the Decree on the Ministry and Life of Priests. Except for the Decree on the Instruments of Social Communication these first two documents represent probably the most debatable and controversial areas of the Second Vatican Council.

Nevertheless—and perhaps for this very reason—the matter of Christian education as projected in these two documents should be given careful consideration. There is much here which is fundamental to basic Christian education; there are other matters which are worth investigation; and there are some things recorded here which are rejected in certain educational circles. This should not encourage us to pass over these documents lightly, for Christian education is basic to the Christian cause particularly as it relates to parents, the home, both parochial and public schools, to adult education, to college, graduate, and seminary training.

# I. THE CATHOLIC VIEW ON EDUCATION AND PRIESTLY TRAINING

Both of these documents were promulgated by Pope Paul VI on October 28, 1965.

In the Introduction to the Declaration on Christian Education *(Gravissimum Educationis),* it is pointed out that today the circumstances of our time have made it both more urgent to educate young people and to continue the education of adults. People are more aware of their own dignity and position; they want and demand better education in order to fulfill their proper function in society. Therefore the rights of education—particularly the primary rights of children and parents—are being proclaimed and recognized in public documents and practice.

The Declaration, noting this educational development in the secular world, indicates that "a true education aims at the formation of the human person with respect to his ultimate goal, and simultaneously with respect to the good of those societies of which, as man, he is a member, and in whose responsibilities, as an adult, he will share." (Art. 1.)

Therefore, according to the Second Vatican Council, the latest advances in education should be utilized to give the person the best possible training, including a "positive and prudent sexual education." Moreover, strong moral and religious elements must be introduced into education.

"This sacred Ecumenical Synod has carefully considered the paramount importance of education in the life of man, and its ever-mounting influence on the social progress of this age. In fact, the education of the young and even a measure of continued instruction for adults have grown both easier and more urgent in the circumstances of our times. For as men grow more conscious of their dignity and calling, they prefer to take an increasingly active part in the life of society, especially in economic and political matters. Enjoying more leisure, as they sometimes do, men find that remarkable developments in technology and in scientific investigation, and new means of social communication offer them readier opportunities for attaining their inheritance of intellectual and spiritual culture, and for fulfilling themselves and one another by forging stronger bonds between various groups and even whole peoples." (Introduction.)

Christian education is especially stressed since every Christian, having become "a new creature by rebirth from water and the Holy Spirit, so that he may be called what he truly is, a child of God, is entitled to a Christian education." (Art. 2.) And because parents have given children their life, they are bound "by the most solemn obligation" to educate their offspring—and therefore must be recognized as the primary and principal educators. The Christian family is the first school in the process of Christian education.

Moreover, the family, which has the primary duty of imparting education, needs the help of the whole community. Civil society, according to the document, is to promote the education of youth in many ways such as the following:

1. Protect the duties and rights of parents and others who share in education and to give their aid.

2. According to the principle of subsidiarity, when the endeavors of parents and other societies are lacking, to carry out the work of education in accordance with the wishes of the parents.

3. As the common good demands, to build "schools and institutes."

Besides the family and civil society the Church itself has a duty to provide Christian education. "As a mother the Church is bound to give these children of hers the kind of education through which their entire lives can be penetrated with the spirit of Christ." (Art. 3.) This kind of education will involve catechetical instruction, uses of the media of communications, various groups for mental and physical development, youth associations, and, most important of all, schools.

Parents, who have "the first and inalienable duty and right" to educate their children, must enjoy according to

the Declaration "true freedom in their choice of schools."
It says:

"Consequently, public authority, which has the
obligation to oversee and defend the liberties of
citizens, ought to see to it, out of a concern for dis-
tributive justice, that public subsidies are allocated
in such a way that, when selecting schools for their
children, parents are genuinely free to follow their
consciences.

"For the rest, it is incumbent upon the state to
provide all citizens with the opportunity to acquire an
appropriate degree of cultural enrichment, and with
the proper preparation for exercising their civic duties
and rights. Therefore, the state itself ought to protect
the right of children to receive an adequate schooling.
It should be vigilant about the ability of teachers and
the excellence of their training. It should look after
the health of students and, in general, promote the
whole school enterprise. But it must keep in mind the
principle of subsidiarity, so that no kind of school
monopoly arises. For such a monopoly would militate
against the native rights of the human person, the
development and spread of culture itself, the peaceful
association of citizens, and the pluralism which exists
today in very many societies." (Art. 6.)

It is emphasized that the Church must help all those of
her children who are being educated in schools which are
not Catholic. This is to be done by the witness of the lives
of those who teach in public schools, by the "apostolic
activity" of their fellow-students, and by the ministry of
priests and laymen who give them "the doctrine of salvation" in a way suited to their age and circumstances.
Parents are urged to demand of the state such aids.

The Church has a special duty to develop Catholic
schools which will cultivate the best of secular life along
with spiritual principles. It thus serves as an aid to the
fulfillment of the mission of the People of God and to the
fostering of the dialogue between the Church and mankind. "Consequently, this sacred Synod proclaims anew a
right already made clear in numerous documents of the
Church's teaching authority, namely, the Church's right
freely to establish and to run schools of every kind and at

every level. At the same time, the Council recalls that the exercise of this right makes a supreme contribution to freedom of conscience, the protection of parental rights, and the progress of culture itself." (Art. 8.)

Although the Catholic school is permitted to take on different forms in keeping with local circumstances, nevertheless "all schools which are in any way dependent on the Church should conform" (Art. 9) to the principles declared by the Council. These schools must not only include primary and secondary education, but also professional and technical schools, centers for educating adults and promoting social welfare, for the retarded, and for the preparation of teachers for religious instruction and other types of education. The Church is also concerned with schools of a higher level—especially colleges and universities. In these colleges and universities secular knowledge and Christian faith are to be blended in such a way that there will be a deeper realization of the harmony of faith and science.

In Catholic universities where there is no faculty of sacred theology it is urged that an institute or chair of sacred theology should be established. In non-Catholic universities it is recommended that there should be associations and centers under Catholic auspices "where priests, religious, and laymen who have been judiciously chosen and trained" (Art. 10) should give abiding spiritual and intellectual assistance to university youth. Both in Catholic and non-Catholic universities young people of special promise, particularly in teaching or research, should be helped.

Article 12 of the Declaration stresses the need for cooperation between Catholic schools, and between these and other schools, in order that collaboration should be developed for the good of all mankind. Moreover, universities should work together "to promote international conferences, allot fields of scientific research, share discoveries, exchange teachers temporarily, and foster among themselves whatever else contributes to more helpful service."

In conclusion the Declaration has a final word directed toward young people themselves and to their teachers:

"This sacred Synod urgently implores young people themselves to be aware of the excellence of the teaching vocation, and to be ready to undertake it with a generous spirit, especially in those parts of the globe where a shortage of teachers is causing a crisis in the training of the young.

"This same Synod acknowledges its profound gratitude toward those priests, religious men and women, and lay people who in their evangelical self-dedication devote themselves to the surpassing work of education, including every kind and grade of schooling. It entreats them to carry on magnanimously in their chosen task and to strive to excel in penetrating their students with the spirit of Christ, in the art of teaching, and in the advancement of knowledge. Thus, they will not only foster the internal renewal of the Church, but will safeguard and intensify her beneficial presence in the world of today, especially the world of the intellect." (Conclusion.)

The second document to be considered in this chapter, the Decree on Priestly Formation (*Optatam Totius*), points out that the desired renewal of the Church depends to a great extent on the ministry of priests. Therefore it proclaims the extreme importance of priestly training and lays down certain basic principles to accomplish such a training. It also stresses the virtue of Christian vocations and urges families, teachers, bishops, and all the faithful to promote vocations.

Chapters III and IV deal with the establishment of seminaries and the careful development of spiritual training in these seminaries. The question of celibacy is dealt with as follows:

"Seminarians should be duly aware of the duties and dignity of Christian marriage, which bodies forth the love between Christ and the Church (cf. Eph. 5:32 f.). Let them perceive as well the superiority of virginity consecrated to Christ, so that by a choice which is maturely thought out and magnanimous they may attach themselves to God by a total gift of body and soul.

"Let them be warned of the very severe dangers with which their chastity will be confronted in present-day society. Aided by appropriate helps, both divine and human, may they learn so to integrate the renunciation of marriage into their life and activity that these will not suffer any detriment from celibacy; rather, that they themselves may achieve a greater mastery of soul and body, and added growth in maturity; and may comprehend more profoundly the blessedness promised by the gospel." (Ch. IV, Art. 10.)

Seminary students are to be trained not only in the basic norms of Christian education, but these are to be complemented by the newer findings of sound psychology and pedagogy. The purpose of this is to develop in the students "a due degree of human maturity" which is evident in 1) stability of mind, 2) an ability to make weighty decisions, and 3) a sound evaluation of men and events. Strength of character for justice, fidelity to one's promises, refinement in manners, modesty in speech coupled with charity, are to be formed within the lives of the theological students.

"Let discipline be exercised, then, in a way which will develop in the students an internal attitude by which the authority of superiors will be accepted through an act of personal conviction, that is, conscientiously (cf. Rom. 13:5) and for supernatural reasons. The rules of discipline should be applied in accord with the age of the students so that they can gradually learn to govern themselves, to make wise use of their freedom, to act on their own initiative and energetically, and can know how to work along with their confreres and lay people as well." (Ch. IV, Art. 11.)

The whole pattern of seminary life, which is to be permeated with a desire for piety, silence, and a careful concern for mutual help, must be so arranged, according to the Second Vatican Council, that it provides an initiation into the future life which the priest will lead.

In Chapter V, on the revision of ecclesiastical studies, it is pointed out that before beginning specifically ecclesiastical subjects, theological students should be equipped with the kind of humanistic and scientific training which young men in their own countries receive as a foundation for graduate studies. They are to have a knowledge of Latin, along with the liturgical language proper to each rite. A suitable knowledge of the languages of the Bible and tradition should be encouraged.

When ecclesiastical studies are revised the aim should be first of all, according to this Decree, that the philosophical and theological disciplines be more suitably aligned. And the philosophical disciplines are to be taught in such a manner that the students are led to acquire a solid and coherent knowledge of man, of the world, and of God. In the cultivation of "a love for seeking, honoring, and defending the truth" (Art. 15) the theological student is to be led into a strong personal faith in both God and man.

> "Under the light of faith and with the guidance of the Church's teaching authority, theology should be taught in such a way that students will accurately draw Catholic doctrine from divine revelation, understand that doctrine profoundly, nourish their own spiritual lives with it, and be able to proclaim it, unfold it, and defend it in their priestly ministry.
>
> "In the study of sacred Scripture, which ought to be the soul of all theology, students should be trained with special diligence. After a suitable introduction to it, they should be accurately initiated into exegetical method, grasp the pre-eminent themes of divine revelation, and take inspiration and nourishment from reading and meditating on the sacred books day by day." (Ch. V, Art. 16.)

In regard to dogmatic theology the Second Vatican Council, in the Decree on Priestly Formation, indicates that biblical themes should be considered first of all. Then the Fathers of the Eastern and Western Church are to be studied, followed by the general history of the Church, and the mysteries of salvation under the guidance of St. Thomas Aquinas.

Also in the renewal of theological training special care is to be given to moral theology. In addition such items as canon law, sacred liturgy, and the churches and ecclesial communities separated from the Apostolic Roman See, are to have a place in the curriculum, along with a study of other religions.

Dr. Karl Rahner, S.J., one of the great theologians of the Roman Catholic Church, at the International Conference on the Main Theological Issues of Vatican II, held at the University of Notre Dame in 1966, in a paper entitled "The Task of Theology After the II Vatican Council," declared:

> "Perhaps I am wrong, but I feel that the description of the moral theology of the future in the decree concerning the formation of priests is a severe but just criticism of the moral theology taught in many seminaries. The Decree understands the task and method of moral theology different from that which hitherto has been actually practiced. It would be an obvious and tempting yet, for the future, momentous error to think that the paramount task of systematic theology of the next decade would be a commentary on conciliar text, the historical justification and systematic deepening of the themes explicitly treated by the Council. Such a development of theology in the near future would completely contradict the spirit and intention of the Council. The Council did not want to invite theology to become the means and mode of an introversion of the Church to Herself. The Council wanted an inexorable and, at the same time, courageous confrontation of the Church with our time."

In a paper at this Notre Dame International Conference on the Main Theological Issues of Vatican II (1966), Bishop Christopher Butler, O.S.B., spoke on "The Aggiornamento of Vatican II." After explaining that *aggiornamento* means etymologically "a bringing up-to-date," he proceeded to explain how this was accomplished at the Council and how it must be maintained in the post-conciliar era. After declaring that the conference was not to be retrospective, but to understand Vatican II "as a step toward the future" and to take into consideration the "theory of development" he said: "The Spirit bloweth where it listeth, and it is impossible to foretell, from the present state and condition of the Church, what her history in the coming generations will be. But at least for the moment, without rejecting or denying her past, without any surrender of her patrimony, she appears to have changed her course."

In regard to more "practical" matters it is advocated that teaching methods are to be revised both as regards lectures, discussions, and seminars, and also the development of study on the part of the students—whether privately or in small groups. Excessive multiplication of courses and lectures is to be avoided. Moreover, those questions which retain little significance (or which ought to be left for higher academic studies) are not to be a part of theological studies.

Students studying for the ministry must be personally committed to Christ. They are to venerate with a filial trust the Virgin Mary, and those practices of piety long a part of the usage of the Church are to be zealously cultivated. They must be formed in priestly obedience and be absolutely loyal to the life of the whole Church. "Seminarians should be thoroughly penetrated by the mystery of the Church, especially as it has been presented with clarity by this holy Synod. Thus, bound even now to Christ's Vicar with humble and filial love, attached after ordination to their own bishop as loyal assistants, and working in concert with their brother priests, they will give witness to that unity by which men are attracted to Christ." (Chap. IV, Art. 9.)

The Decree on the Ministry and Life of Priests (*Presbyterorum Ordinis*) was promulgated by Pope Paul VI on December 7, 1965, and is closely related to the Decree on Priestly Formation in that it not only deals with the priesthood in the mission of the Church, in the relationship of priests to the People of God and particularly to bishops, but also to the entire training and daily life of priests.

One of the key passages of this important document is that stressing the unique powers granted through the sacrament of ordination to priests:

"Now, the same Lord has established certain ministers among the faithful in order to join them together in one body where 'all the members have not the same function' (Rom. 12:4). These ministers in the society of the faithful would be able by the sacred power of their order to offer sacrifice and to remit sins. They would perform their priestly office publicly for men in the name of Christ.

"So it was that Christ sent the apostles just as He Himself had been sent by the Father. Through these same apostles He made their successors, the bishops, sharers in His consecration and mission. Their ministerial role has been handed down to priests in a limited degree. Thus established in the order of the priesthood, they are co-workers of the episcopal order in the proper fulfillment of the apostolic mission entrusted to the latter order by Christ." (Ch. I, Art. 2.)

Priests, being related to the episcopal order through their bishops, share in the authority by which Christ rules His Church. Being anointed by the Holy Spirit they are marked with a special character and have the power to act in the person of Christ. Through the Mass, and the sacraments, the priest in a very special way brings Christ to the People of God.

## II. FROM THE NON-CATHOLIC VIEWPOINT

Although there are some basic differences in the area of Christian education (which will be considered later in this chapter) between Roman Catholicism and Protestantism, there are as in most other areas many points of agreement. Dr. John C. Bennett, President of Union Theological Seminary, New York City, in his Response to the Declaration on Christian Education (in *The Documents of Vatican II*, pp. 652-655) points out that the statement of the responsibility of the Church, and the outlining of the goals for Christian education are, in the document, in general terms sound.

Dr. Bennett, speaking as a Protestant educator, says, "I am sure that the content of education suggested by such words as 'the formation of the human person with respect to the ultimate goal' would involve great differences of emphasis among Christians and not necessarily as between Catholics and Protestants. Also, in general terms, the right things are said about the effect of Christian education on the relation between Catholics and other Christians, and between Christians and non-Christians. The need of relating Christian education to a pluralistic society is recognized. Also, the responsibility of that society to provide education for all children as a matter of justice is given the emphasis that it deserves."

Both Protestants and members of the Orthodox churches today, in such a pluralistic society as we have in the

United States, agree in the main with the following positions taken in the Declaration:

1. The rights and responsibility of parents for the education of their children.

2. A check on the secular emphasis that the government, or the community acting through the agencies of the state, is the educator.

3. The responsibility of the state both to make sure that children have opportunities for education and to set standards.

4. The right to have both public and parochial schools.

5. Some adjustment to supporting parochial schools in areas which do not come under any kind of religious control or discipline.

6. The support of "shared time."

7. Giving Catholic parochial students exactly the same type of welfare benefits as are given to all other students by the government, whether local, state, or national.

In the realm of theological education there is much identical material used by both Protestants and Catholics, although much greater stress is placed upon dogma, rules, and regulations by Catholic seminaries. As a result of the Second Vatican Council much greater attention will now be placed upon Protestant and Orthodox teaching (along with non-Christian teaching) and Catholic and Protestant seminaries are already exchanging both teachers and students for specialized courses. Moreover, biblical scholars and theological professors of both sides today have many projects in common and the contribution of scholars at the Second Vatican Council, those of a progressive nature, have brought the teaching of seminaries much closer together.

One of the major differences in the ecumenical movement is the issue of government support of religious private schools—Catholic, Orthodox, or Protestant. Here the sides are not clearly drawn. Some Protestants, for example, support state aid for parochial schools; some Catholics do not. Many Protestants do not object to supplying government aid for specific welfare benefits to all children, in both private and public schools; many Catholics hold the same position. Both, however, in many cases, object to giving government financial support directly to private religious schools.

American bishops of the Catholic Church took active

leadership in getting the Declaration on Religious Freedom through the Second Vatican Council. On other occasions they have supported in liberty the principle of the First Amendment to the United States Constitution. They want a separation of Church and State here in the United States. Yet when it comes to the interpretation of the meaning of the separation of Church and State, especially as it concerns financial aid to parochial schools, there is a vast amount of confusion and misunderstanding.

The Second Vatican Council, at certain points, declared for direct support of Roman Catholic schools by the government, financially and otherwise. Most Protestants, as well as many Roman Catholics in this country, are not able in good conscience to support such a proposition. They are convinced that although the Church and State must co-operate in certain areas, the Church must never, through financial favors, come under the domination of the State. They believe that it is good both for the Church and the State to have separate powers and authority each in their own respective areas. They believe that when the State takes over the functions of the Church, in one way or another, then the Church loses its prophetic power and ceases to be a true Church.

Most Protestants, and probably most Catholics in the United States, seem to agree with this statement by Justice William O. Douglas of the United States Supreme Court in *The Bible and the Schools* (Little, Brown, 1966, p. 58): "Christianity has sufficient inner strength to survive and flourish on its own. It does not need state subsidies, nor state privileges, nor state prestige. The more it obtains state support the greater it curtails human freedom."

The position of non-Catholics toward public and parochial schools is stated briefly in this 1965 General Board resolution of the National Council of Churches in the U.S.A.: "The General Board of the National Council of Churches has repeatedly expressed its support for public education and urged that federal aid be given to public schools throughout the nation. All the children have a right to share in this aid through attendance at public schools. To the extent compatible with the religion clauses of the First Amendment and the sound principle of public control of public funds, those attending private and parochial schools should benefit from this aid."

The National Council of Churches, in this same resolution, went on record supporting "dual school enrollment"—whereby children of parochial schools share on a part-time basis the instruction and facilities of public schools—as "an effective and appropriate way" to have all children benefit from special federal aid. Then it adds, "This arrangement is a more acceptable mode of benefiting all children than arrangements under which payments from public funds would be made directly to private and parochial schools or parents."

Dr. Arthur S. Flemming, first vice-president of the National Council of Churches, and former Secretary of the United States Department of Health, Education, and Welfare (and at present President of Oregon State University), in testifying before the House and Senate subcommittee hearings on the Elementary and Secondary Education Act of 1965, indicated that in advocating the dual system the Council had not changed its position regarding direct federal aid to parochial schools. He said that "a program for making federal grants to the private schools would be opposed vigorously by many of the member communions of the National Council."

Dr. Flemming, in the name of the National Council, then proceeded to state the following safeguards in connection with the use of public funds to assist students in private schools:

"1. That benefits for students not include 'grants' from federal, state or local tax funds for non-public elementary and secondary schools.

"2. That benefits for students must be determined and administered by public authorities.

"3. That the benefits for students should be identifiable by the students as public services.

"4. That the benefit program not be used directly or indirectly for the inculcation of religion or the teaching of sectarian doctrine.

"5. That, in the administration of a benefit program, there be no discrimination by reason of race, religion, class, or national origin in the distribution of the benefits.

"6. That 'funds should be administered by the states with provision for reports to the Commissioner of Education on the use of the funds.' "

Many feel that if all private and parochial schools, both Catholic and non-Catholic, would keep within these guidelines there would be little or no opposition from Protestants. It is only when Catholic school officials and high-pressure organizations begin to clamor for full state and federal aid out of public tax funds that both Protestant and secular forces begin to object seriously. When this is done, and public funds are granted to religious schools, these non-Catholic forces feel very strongly that the basic principle of the separation of Church and State is being violated. And such a violation, they maintain, hurts everybody (including both Church and State) in the long run.

Largely as a result of the Second Vatican Council, especially its Decree on Ecumenism, the whole matter of Christian education and in particular parochial schools is being carefully re-examined. Some of the reasons for separate religious schools no longer exist. There is now no longer a need to keep Catholic students from co-mingling with Protestant students. Now the time has come to make all of life *Christian*—using the educational facilities of the home, the church, and the school—not only during childhood and youth, but all through life.

Here, therefore, is the challenge facing Catholics and non-Catholics working together in the new ecumenical frame of reference: how to create a total educational system which will preserve all that is best and vital in religion within the basic principles of the separation of Church and State. As the spirit of Vatican II actually gets down to the community level we may, in time, realize a new type of joint educational system where doctrine will not be compromised, but where practice will follow the guidelines of creative ecumenism.

## III. QUESTIONS FOR DISCUSSION

1. How does Christian education differ among Roman Catholics, Eastern Orthodox, and Protestants?

2. Just what is the purpose of Christian education?

3. Should the government use public tax funds to support parochial (religious) schools?

4. What is the difference in the training of priests and ministers in the Roman Catholic Church and the Protestant churches?

5. Does sex education have a real place in the curriculum of our church schools?

6. How can Catholics, Protestants, and members of the Orthodox churches cooperate in the area of education?

7. How can religious education be applied to adults as well as children and young people?

8. Is it possible to remove all religious bias and prejudice from our church school textbooks?

## IV. SUGGESTIONS FOR ECUMENICAL ACTION

1. Read the Declaration on Christian Education, the Decree on Priestly Formation, and the Decree on the Ministry and Life of Priests in *The Documents of Vatican II*.

2. Find out how much tax money is being spent in your community on Protestant, Catholic, Orthodox, and Jewish schools.

3. Visit a parochial school.

4. (Protestant) Ask a Roman Catholic priest to give you a review of his theological training. (Catholic) Ask a Protestant pastor to give you a review of his theological training.

5. Talk with a public school principal about the value of "shared time."

6. Discover any new developments in adult religious education.

"By divine favor, especially in modern times, human genius has produced from natural material astonishing inventions in the field of technology. Some of these have extraordinary bearing on the human spirit, since they open up new and highly effective avenues of communication for all kinds of information, ideas, and directives." (Decree on the Instruments of Social Communication, Art. 1.)

## CHAPTER IX

# Communicating the Gospel

## INTRODUCTION

The Decree on the Instruments of Social Communication (*Inter Mirifica*) was promulgated by Pope Paul VI on December 4, 1963. While it may be the weakest of all the sixteen documents of the Second Vatican Council, nevertheless it should be carefully studied not only to discover what it does say, but also to ascertain what it has left unsaid and where it has fallen short of the mark. For, as is pointed out in the Introduction of the document, the Church realizes that such media as the press, radio, and television if properly used can "contribute generously to the refreshment and refinement of the spirit, and to the spread and strengthening of God's own kingdom." (Art. 2.) On the other hand, when poorly used, or used in direct opposition to the spirit and aims of the Church, these media can do much harm to individuals and to society.

## I. THE POSITION OF THE CHURCH ON COMMUNICATION

The first chapter of the Decree on the Instruments of

Social Communication begins with the statement that the "Catholic Church has been commissioned by the Lord Christ to bring salvation to every man, and is consequently bound to proclaim the gospel. Hence she judges it part of her duty to preach the news of redemption with the aid of the instruments of social communication, and to instruct mankind as well in their worthy use." (Art. 3.)

It then goes on to say that it is "a birthright" of the Church to have at its disposal and to employ any of these media insofar as they are necessary or useful for the instruction of Christians and for all its efforts for the welfare of souls. Moreover, it states that it is the duty of pastors to instruct and guide the faithful so that they may, with the help of such media, further the salvation and perfection both of themselves and of the entire human family.

It adds that the laity also must especially strive to instill a human and Christian spirit into these media so that they may "abundantly satisfy the high hopes of mankind and the will of God Himself."

> "If these instruments are to be properly employed, it is absolutely necessary that all who use them know the norms of morality and apply them faithfully in this field. They should, therefore, consider the subject matter, which each instrument will communicate in its own way. At the same time, they should thoughtfully weigh all those circumstantial elements which define an action of communication and can modify its moral quality or even reverse it entirely. These include questions of intention, audience, place, and time." (Ch. I, Art. 4.)

The decree then deals with three questions of our day which need the guidance of a proper moral outlook:

1. The first has to do with the search for and the reporting of the news.

2. The second deals with the relationship "between what is called art and the rights and norms of the moral law." (Art. 6.)

3. The third points out that the narration, description, or portrayal of moral evil, even through the media of social communication "can indeed serve to make man more deeply known and studied, and to reveal and enhance the grandeur of truth and goodness. Such aims are

achieved by means of appropriately heightened dramatic effects." (Art. 7.)

"Today public opinion exerts massive force and authority over the private and public life of every class of citizen. Hence the necessity arises for every member of society to do what justice and charity require in this matter. With the aid of these instruments, then, each man should strive to form and to voice worthy views on public affairs." (Art. 8.)

Stress is placed upon striving for moral goodness on the part of those who produce programs for radio, TV, and motion pictures, and also in the area of the arts. Moreover, those who listen and view must keep the matter of morality in mind. This is especially true in respect to youth.

Public authority (or the secular government) is said to have special responsibilities in the realm of mass communications.

> "In this whole field, civil authority is bound by special duties in terms of the common good, to which these instruments are subordinate. This authority is duty bound to defend and protect a true and just availability of information; the progress of modern society utterly depends on this, especially as regards freedom of the press. This authority should foster religion, culture, and fine arts; it should protect consumers in the free exercise of their lawful rights. It should also assist the undertaking of projects which could not otherwise be initiated, despite their extreme usefulness, especially for young people.

> "Finally public authority, which properly concerns itself with the health of its citizens, has the duty of seeing to it in a just and vigilant manner that serious danger to public morals and social progress do not result from a perverted use of these instruments. This goal should be achieved by enactment of laws and their energetic enforcement. The freedom of individuals and groups is not at all infringed upon by such watchful care, especially if those who have taken on themselves the responsibility of using these media have failed to observe sensible cautions.

> "Particular effort should be expended to protect youngsters from literature and shows which would be injurious to them at their age." (Art. 12.)

The second chapter of the document deals with the pastoral activity of the Church in relation to social communication. Pastors are urged to fulfill their duty in this respect. The laity are encouraged to make use of the media in order to bear "witness to Christ." A truly Catholic press should be established to "publicize and correctly interpret facts which pertain to the life of the Church." (Art. 14.) Catholic radio and TV programs should be developed. Catholic radio and TV stations should be constructed. Catholic priests, religious, and laymen ought to be afforded technical training in all aspects of mass media. Instruction in the proper use of the media should be given in Catholic schools at every level. And each year in every diocese the Catholic faithful should be given the opportunity to pray and contribute funds for the benefit of Catholic media of social communication.

The Decree points out that the Sovereign Pontiff has a special office of the Holy See in relation to social communication. It also adds that the Council would like to see this Secretariat enlarged in its scope with experts from various countries named to it, including laymen. Besides, it orders that a series of national offices for affairs of the press, films, radio, and television be established everywhere and given every aid. These national offices have the special task "of helping the faithful to form a true conscience about the use of these media, and of fostering and coordinating Catholic activities directed to this end." (Art. 21.) These offices are to be entrusted to a special committee of bishops (or a single bishop) with laymen who are experts in Catholic teaching and in these arts or techniques having some role in the offices. They also are to be coordinated on an international plane with other Catholic organizations dealing in this area. "These groups are only those lawfully endorsed by the Holy See and responsible to it." (Art. 22.)

"This sacred Synod trusts that all the sons of the Church will cordially welcome and religiously observe this program of precepts and guidelines. By so doing they will not only avoid harm in the use of these advantages, but they will season the earth as its salt, and illumine the world as its light.

"The Council further entreats all men of good will, especially those who control these instruments, to strive to apply them solely for the good of mankind. The fate of humanity grows daily more dependent on the right use of these media. And so, as with ancient artistic achievements, the name of the Lord will be glorified by these modern inventions as well. Thus will be fulfilled that ideal of the Apostle: 'Jesus Christ yesterday, today, yes, and forever' (Heb. 13:8)." (Art. 24.)

## II. THE PROTESTANT AND ORTHODOX POSITIONS

In regard to this Decree there is no Catholic or Protestant or Orthodox position. Communications, particularly in relation to the mass media, is a modern phenomenon and relates to the secular rather than to theology. In practice Protestantism has made greater use of the press, radio, and TV than either Roman Catholicism or the Orthodox Church, although the former, through the Second Vatican Council, gained tremendous momentum. As to the Decree itself there was strong Protestant opposition all along the line; but there was also as strong opposition from many Fathers of the Council. Therefore, this document does not lend itself to an *either-or* criticism, but rather to a *both-and* analysis.

Because this whole area of public relations and the creative use of the means of modern communications is so essential to the "image" and to the extension of the good news of Christ through the world, in terms of knowledge and evangelism, this Decree should be taken seriously, although quite inadequate.

The Second Vatican Council, because it was the greatest religious event of the century, commanded an unprecedented amount of attention from mass communications. Because it was new, and constantly creative, it made news. And although the press relations at the Second Vatican Council at the beginning left just about everything to be desired, by the time of the second session an extensive and smooth-running public relations operation had been worked out.

At hardly any other point does the Church reach the general public to a greater extent than through the media of the press, popular magazines, radio, and television. It is therefore imperative that the Church have good public relations in order to tell its message adequately to the modern world.

It is also essential, if the documents of the Second Vatican Council are to be seriously implemented, to make the best possible use of mass media.

This Decree on the Instruments of Social Communication admits all this. But when it comes to providing a blueprint or a guideline for the future, this document fails almost completely. Such a failure is not in keeping with the progressive spirit of the Council. Yet this is not all. The document is so reactionary at specific points that— set in the twentieth century—it is filled with great potential danger both to the Church and to society as a whole. This is why the document was opposed so vigorously up to the very day of promulgation.

Assuming that the promulgation did not alter the basic objections raised against the document by bishops of the Council and numerous *periti,* and by a number of observers, these criticisms ought still to be carefully considered. When it was realized that this "weak" document had hidden in it several points of potential danger, five Council Fathers signed a circular headed *URGENTE* asking the Council to vote *"non placet"* on the communications schema on November 25, 1963.

Criticism of the final version of the document was summed up in a statement issued by three prominent Roman Catholic (American) newsmen. The statement was also countersigned by four notable theologians: Father John Courtney Murray, S.J., Father Jean Danielou, S.J., Father Jorge Mejia, S.J., and Father Bernard Haring, C.SS.R., with the words "This statement is worthy of consideration." The statement claimed that the Decree was "not an *aggiornamento,* but a step backward," and declared that where the document was "not vague and banal, it reflects a hopelessly abstract view of the relationship of the Church and modern culture. It deals with a press that exists only in textbooks and is unrecognizable to us." After making a number of specific points for censure it asserted, finally, that "it may one day be cited as a classic example of how the Second Vatican Council failed to come to grips with the world around it."

One observer wrote a bill of particulars against it and another observer sent a letter to Augustin Cardinal Bea asking him to take some steps, as head of the Secretariat for the Promotion of Christian Unity, to block action on the document.

Nevertheless, despite hundreds of objections, the document became, as Father Gustave Weigel, S.J., described it, the "official and authentic doctrine of the Church," although it did not and would not become the "irreformable and once-for-all-times doctrine of the Church." With this hopeful sign in mind, let us look at some of the potential danger spots in this Decree on the Instruments of Social Communication.

Here are the specific dangers represented in this document:

—All (Roman Catholic and non-Catholic) who use the instruments of mass communication *must* meet the (Roman Catholic) Church's stand as to what constitutes a "correct conscience," or take the consequences.

—Censorship is definitely indicated: news can be censored if it does not edify and art can be suppressed if it does not teach.

—Novels and plays which do not at all times teach a particular and precise kind of moral rectitude dictated by the Church are inadmissible.

—The opinion of competent "authorities" must be sought by all those who read books, watch plays and television, and listen to radio: a directive which implies the rights of censorship, boycott, and reprisals.

—It is the obligation of the Church to protect and insulate youth from all possible contamination in the area of mass media, rather than to help young people develop their own criteria of judgment.

—The reporting of Church news must not be critical of the Church.

—State (national) authorities must legislate widely in the area of the *morals* of mass communication, with the direct implication that the Church dictates the proper moral standards.

—Roman Catholics are encouraged to establish a *Catholic* press, *Catholic* radio, *Catholic* TV, rather than trying to raise the general level of all mass communications.

—All that Roman Catholics do in the field of mass communications—such as having their own stations and developing programing—should be under the strict supervision of Roman Catholic "authorities."

All this is contrary to the progressive spirit of the Council itself and is in direct opposition to the development of a strong, creative mass communication system serving the general public as well as the best interests of the Church. It does not take into account the fact that mass communication is now composed of several professional groups of high standing which are extremely sensitive concerning their own standards. In this group there are Catholics, Protestants, Anglicans, Jews, and those without any definite religious affiliation. The professionals are not thinking in sectarian terms, but in terms of how they can gather, write, and project the news as *news*. They react instantly to any suggestion of censorship, management of news, or the curtailment in any degree of the freedom of the press.

The only way in which the document can contribute to this professional feeling is for the Church to take seriously the objections filed by the members of the working press, and especially by those who are members of the Roman Catholic Church, who plainly and openly declare that the document represents the status quo and that a new development must take place in regard to mass communications in the post-conciliar period. It is greatly encouraging to know that there is a segment of the Church which really knows the score in this area and has the "know-how" to produce better mass communications now and for the future.

Here is an area of ecumenical relations where the Church can make its greatest contributions by leaving off the "Catholic" label. Moreover, if this is done, there are possibilities of ecumenical relationships in mass communication (such as *Religion in American Life*)[1] which challenge the imagination.

# III. QUESTIONS FOR DISCUSSION

1. Why is this document on communications considered by both Catholics and Protestants to be the weakest of the sixteen documents of Vatican II?

---

[1] *Religion in American Life* is an interfaith organization, with national headquarters at 184 Fifth Avenue, New York, which promotes the cause of religion through the mass media.

2. What are the Catholic and Protestant positions in regard to censorship?

3. What has happened to the *Index* of prohibited books?

4. How does the Roman Catholic Church make especially good use of the mass media?

5. When should there be interfaith cooperation in mass communication?

6. Where can the priest or minister receive the best training in the art and techniques of mass communication?

7. Why is it difficult to have freedom of communication in any form of a church-state?

8. What is the best way for Protestants, Catholics, and the Orthodox to cooperate in the development of decent movies, books, and plays?

9. In what ways are Catholics going beyond the Decree on the Instruments of Social Communication?

# IV. SUGGESTIONS FOR ECUMENICAL ACTION

1. Study the Decree on the Instruments of Social Communication as found in *The Documents of Vatican II.*

2. Read several reviews of plays, TV programs, movies in Roman Catholic and Protestant magazines or papers.

3. Find out what is actually involved in the words *Nihil Obstat* and *Imprimatur* used in relation to Catholic books.

4. Check to see what has now taken the place of the Roman Catholic *Index* of prohibited books.

5. Compare, over a period of a month, the amount of space given in your local paper to Catholic news in comparison to that given to Protestant news.

6. Note the number of "ecumenical" programs over TV within a certain period of time (a month or six months).

# PART FOUR

# Implementation: Of Conscience and Renewal

"The Church does not deal with the secular order in terms of a double standard—freedom for the Church when Catholics are a minority, privilege for the Church and intolerance for others when Catholics are a majority."

—*Father John Courtney Murray, S.J., in his introduction to the Declaration on Religious Freedom in* The Documents of Vatican II. (p. 673.)

"A sense of the dignity of the human person has been impressing itself more and more deeply on the consciousness of contemporary man. And the demand is increasingly made that men should act on their own judgment, enjoying and making use of a responsible freedom, not driven by coercion but motivated by a sense of duty. The demand is also made that constitutional limits should be set to the powers of government, in order that there may be no encroachment on the rightful freedom of the person and of associations." (Introduction to the Declaration on Religious Freedom, Art. 1.)

CHAPTER X

# The Rights of Conscience

## INTRODUCTION

Father John Courtney Murray, S.J., the chief architect of the Declaration on Religious Freedom of the Second Vatican Council, at the International Conference on the Theological Issues of Vatican II held at the University of Notre Dame, March 20-26, 1966, pointed out the fact that this Declaration not only is a major achievement of the Council, but if it had not been adopted, for one reason or another, the results would have been disastrous.

While there is nothing essentially new in it, and while it had a rather difficult time getting through the Council, the promulgation of the Declaration on Religious Freedom (*Dignitatis Humanae*) by Pope Paul VI on December 7, 1965, represented a great historic milestone in the life of the Roman Catholic Church. What it did was to bring this Church up-to-date; the Church by adopting this Declaration on Religious Freedom took a step forward in order to catch up with mankind. It was indeed an act of sincere humility.

Here the Church admitted its tardiness and also its debt to the progress already made by the civilized world.

# I. FROM THE VATICAN II POINT OF VIEW

The document begins with the statement that the dignity of the human person has been impressing itself more and more deeply on the consciousness of modern man and that the demand is increasingly being made that men should act on their own judgment, "enjoying and making use of a responsible freedom, not driven by coercion but motivated by a sense of duty." The demand, it proceeds to say, is likewise made that constitutional limits should be set to the powers of government, in order that there may be no encroachment on the rightful freedom of the person and of various associations of people. While this demand for freedom in human society chiefly regards the quest for the values proper to the human spirit, at the very heart of it is the desire for the free exercise of religion. "This Vatican Synod takes careful note of these desires in the minds of men. It proposes to declare them to be greatly in accord with truth and justice." (Art. 1.)

After emphasizing the point that the "one true religion subsists in the catholic and apostolic Church" and that the Declaration "leaves untouched traditional Catholic doctrine on the moral duty of men and societies toward the true religion and toward the one Church of Christ" (Art. 1), it says:

> "This Vatican Synod declares that the human person has a right to religious freedom. This freedom means that all men are to be immune from coercion on the part of individuals or of social groups and of any human power, in such wise that in matters religious no one is to be forced to act in a manner contrary to his own beliefs. Nor is anyone to be restrained from acting in accordance with his own beliefs, whether privately or publicly, whether alone or in association with others, within due limits.
>
> "The Synod further declares that the right to religious freedom has its foundation in the very dignity of the human person, as this dignity is known through

the revealed word of God and by reason itself. This right of the human person to religious freedom is to be recognized in the constitutional law whereby society is governed. Thus it is to become a civil right." (Ch. I, Art. 2.)

The document then explains, in detail, this fundamental principle of religious liberty. It calls attention to the fact that men cannot discharge their rights and obligations unless they enjoy immunity from external coercion. And it points out that "the right to this immunity continues to exist even in those who do not live up to their obligation of seeking the truth and adhering to it. Nor is the exercise of this right to be impeded, provided that just requirements of public order be observed." (Art. 2.)

It goes on to indicate that man perceives and acknowledges the imperatives of the divine law through the mediation of conscience. Moreover, in all his activity a man is bound to follow his conscience in order that he may come to God. Therefore he cannot be forced to act in a manner contrary to his conscience. In the exercise of religion there must be a basis of internal, voluntary, and free acts. "No merely human power can either command or prohibit acts of this kind." (Art. 3.)

Religious freedom for religious communities (denominations) means this:

1. The right to govern themselves according to their own norms.

2. The right to honor the Supreme Being in public worship.

3. The right to assist their members in the practice of the religious life.

4. The right to strengthen their members by instruction.

5. The right to promote institutions in which they may join together for the purpose of ordering their own lives in accordance with their religious principles.

6. The right not to be hindered, either by legal measures or by administrative action on the part of the government a) in the selection, training, appointment, and transferral of their own ministers; b) in communicating with religious authorities and communities abroad; c) in erecting buildings for religious purposes; d) in the acquisition and use of suitable funds or properties.

7. The right not to be hindered in their public teaching

and witness to their faith, whether by the spoken or by the written word.

8. The right not to be prohibited from freely undertaking to show the special value of their doctrine to society and of the whole human activity.

9. The right freely to hold meetings and to establish educational, cultural, charitable, and social organizations, under the impulse of their own religious sense.

10. The right of the family freely to live its own domestic religious life under the guidance of parents.

11. The right of parents to determine, in accordance with their own religious beliefs, the kind of religious education that their children are to receive.

"Government, in consequence, must acknowledge the right of parents to make a genuinely free choice of schools and of other means of education. The use of this freedom of choice is not to be made a reason for imposing unjust burdens on parents, whether directly or indirectly. Besides, the rights of parents are violated if their children are forced to attend lessons or instruction which are not in agreement with their religious beliefs. The same is true if a single system of education, from which all religious formation is excluded, is imposed upon all." (Art. 5.)

According to the Declaration, government is also to help create conditions favorable to the fostering of religious life. This is in order that people may be truly enabled to exercise their religious rights and to fulfill their religious duties. It is also in order that society itself may profit by the moral qualities of justice and peace. Then the Declaration makes this important point: "If, in view of peculiar circumstances obtaining among certain peoples, special legal recognition is given in the constitutional order of society to one religious body, it is at the same time imperative that the right of all citizens and religious bodies to religious freedom should be recognized and made effective in practice." (Art. 6.)

Moreover, it notes, government is to see to it that equality of citizens before the law is never violated, whether openly or covertly, for religious reasons. "Nor is there to be discrimination among citizens."

"It follows that a wrong is done when government imposes upon its people, by force or fear or other means, the profession or repudiation of any religion, or when it hinders men from joining or leaving a religious body. All the more is it a violation of the will of God and of the sacred rights of the person and the family of nations, when force is brought to bear in any way in order to destroy or repress religion, either in the whole of mankind or in a particular country or in a specific community." (Art. 6.)

The Declaration points out that as there are certain rights, there are also certain responsibilities. In several places in the document the phrase "provided just public order is observed" is used. This means, according to the document, that in the employment of all freedoms the moral principle of personal and social responsibility is to be observed. Religious people must have respect for the rights of others. Government has the right to defend itself against possible abuses committed on the pretext of freedom of religion. "For the rest, the usages of society are to be the usages of freedom in their full range. These require that the freedom of man be respected as far as possible, and curtailed only when and in so far as necessary." (Art. 7.)

While religious people should be taught to obey the law and be good citizens for the public good, the matter of conscientious objection, based upon religious principles, is to be protected by law. (This latter point is implied in this Declaration as specified in the Pastoral Constitution on the Church in the Modern World.)

The document ends with Chapter II, supporting religious freedom on the basis of divine revelation in several paragraphs:

1. God calls men to serve Him in spirit and in truth; therefore they are bound in conscience but they stand under no compulsion.

2. Christ refused to impose the truth by force on those who spoke against it.

3. The apostles strove to convert men to faith in Christ, but never by the use of force.

4. The Church throughout the ages "has kept safe and handed on the doctrine received from the Master and from the apostles."

"In the life of the People of God as it has made its pilgrim way through the vicissitudes of human history, there have at times appeared ways of acting which were less in accord with the spirit of the gospel or even opposed to it. Nevertheless, the doctrine of the Church that no one is to be coerced into faith has always stood firm." (Ch. II, Art. 12.)

Because the Church has a command to "teach all nations" (Mt. 28:19-20) it must proceed in freedom to fulfill this commission, and individual members of the Church must be free to help it carry it out. In the modern world most governments give constitutional recognition to religious freedom, as do certain international bodies. But some governments, although having religious freedom written into their constitutions do not allow it in practice.

This important Declaration closes with these words:

"This sacred Synod greets with joy the first of these two facts, as among the signs of the times. With sorrow, however, it denounces the other fact, as only to be deplored. The Synod exhorts Catholics, and it directs a plea to all men, most carefully to consider how greatly necessary religious freedom is, especially in the present condition of the human family.

"All nations are coming into ever closer unity. Men of different cultures and religions are being brought together in closer relations. There is a growing consciousness of the personal responsibility that weighs upon every man. All this is evident.

"Consequently, in order that relationships of peace and harmony be established and maintained within the whole of mankind, it is necessary that religious freedom be everywhere provided with an effective constitutional guarantee, and that respect be shown for the high duty and right of man freely to lead his religious life in society." (Art. 15.)

## II. PROTESTANTS AND RELIGIOUS FREEDOM

A Catholic editor at the Second Vatican Council, when the final vote was taken on the Declaration on Religious Freedom, remarked: "At last, the Roman Catholic Church has caught up with Roger Williams!" Historically there is much truth in this and it was reflected in the fact that the American bishops were the chief proponents of the document, which, by the way, had a difficult time getting born.

To many this document, which went through several revisions, was so essential to the whole ecumenical movement that the success or failure of the Council was related to its passage. If the Council had failed to adopt it, then many Protestants and some cardinals of the Roman Catholic Church would have considered the Council a "failure." This was due to the fact that this was the one essential point where the Church should be brought up to date. Protestants, the United Nations, most governments had already declared the rights of the individual conscience. Now it was time for the Roman Catholic Church to get into line and declare itself publicly and officially.

At New Delhi the World Council of Churches (1961) put it this way:

> "Freedom to manifest one's religion or belief, in public or in private and alone or in community with others, is essential to the expression of inner freedom.
>
> "(a) It includes freedom to worship according to one's chosen form, in public or in private.
>
> "(b) It includes freedom to teach, whether by formal or informal instruction as well as preaching with a view to propagating one's faith and persuading others to accept it.
>
> "(c) It includes freedom to practice religion or belief, whether by performance of acts of mercy or by the expression in word or deed of the implications of belief in social, economic, and political matters, both domestic and international.
>
> "(d) It includes freedom of observance by following religious customs or by participating in religious rites in the family or in public meeting." (*The New Delhi Report,* Association Press, p. 160.)

Father John Courtney Murray said at the Notre Dame theological conference: "Its [the Second Vatican Council's] achievement was simply to bring the Church abreast of the developments that have occurred in the secular world. The fact is the right of men to religious freedom has already been accepted and affirmed by the common consciousness of mankind."

Father John B. Sheerin, C.S.P., editor of *The Catholic World*, says in regard to the Declaration, "The Council document is not at all radical by American standards. With us, religious liberty is a long-standing political reality. To defend religious liberty in America is about as daring and progressive as to defend motherhood."

It is significant, from the Protestant point of view, that Prof. Thomas T. Love of Cornell College, who has made a special study of religious liberty, has said, "The approval of *De Libertate Religiosa* at the fourth session of Vatican Council II was an historical occasion of singular significance. The Roman Catholic Church finally declared itself unequivocally in favor of the civil right to religious freedom for all persons." Although he considers the declaration to be "a somewhat ambiguous and unsystematic statement," he nevertheless considers it "a monumental accomplishment." And while he is not blind to the emphasis in it on the "one true Church," he considers the fact that in its doctrinal development the Roman Catholic Church has here gone far beyond the toleration of error, to the position that even error has civil rights (or the persons who hold "errors" have civil rights), is in itself a great accomplishment.

It should be noted that during 1965, when the Second Vatican Council finally voted the Declaration on Religious Freedom, the U.N. Commission on Human Rights and its Subcommittee on the Prevention of Discrimination and the Protection of Minorities, in compliance with a request from the U.N. General Assembly, devoted their session in 1965 to the elaboration of a Draft International Convention on the Elimination of All Forms of Religious Intolerance. Stated in the draft already adopted are these words:

> "*Considering* that the Universal Declaration of Human Rights (1948) proclaims the principle of non-discrimination and the right to freedom of thought, conscience, religion and belief;
> "*Considering* that religion or belief, for anyone who professes either, is a fundamental element in his conception of life, and that freedom to practice religion as well as to manifest a belief should be fully respected and guaranteed; . . ."

Also in 1965 the Executive Committee of the Commission of the Churches for International Affairs of the World Council of Churches, expressing the hope that the Vatican II Declaration on Religious Freedom will be adopted and promulgated "without any weakening of its content and without any restrictive interpretation," and recalling and reaffirming the views expressed in the Declaration on Religious Liberty adopted at Amsterdam in 1948 by the WCC and the one adopted by the WCC at New Delhi in 1961, went on to say:

"We welcome current efforts to ensure religious liberty and believe that in order that their objective may be fully achieved certain essential requirements should be met, among which we stress the following:

"1. While holding a distinctive Christian basis for religious liberty, the civil freedom which Christians claim for themselves must be guaranteed to all men everywhere, whatever their religion or belief.

"2. Religious liberty includes freedom to change one's religion or belief without consequent social, economic, and political disabilities. Implicit in this right is the right freely to maintain one's belief or disbelief without external coercion or disability."

President John C. Bennett of Union Theological Seminary, New York City, points up some of the fears of Protestants in regard to losing their liberties in the following statement made at a Catholic-sponsored conference on the Christian and Religious Liberty on the American Scene held in the Carnegie International Center in New York City, May 8, 1965. Dr. Bennett said:

"I believe that the American hierarchy has been right in giving so much attention to religious liberty because this has been the deepest source of misunderstanding between Catholics and Protestants in this country. I have found that it is a very common Protestant view of Roman Catholicism that, if the Roman Catholic Church were to be what it really intends to be, it would take as its model the Spanish Church. . . . They cannot be blamed for this because it was very easy to find official Roman Catholic documents which implied this but difficult to find statements that had equal authority which gave reassurance.

Also there was the famous passage in *Catholic Principles of Politics* by John A. Ryan and F. J. Boland which gave the basis for believing that, if the Catholic Church ever came to represent a large majority, it would limit the external expressions of the religious liberty of non-Catholics."

Martin Luther, in his *On Secular Authority*, puts it this way:

"For the Proverb is true, 'thoughts are free.' Why then would they (the rulers) constrain people to believe in their hearts, when they see it is impossible? In this way they compel weak consciences to lie, to deny, and to say what they do not believe in their hearts, and they load themselves down with dreadful alien sins. For all the lies and false confessions which such weak consciences utter fall back upon him who compels them. It were far better, if their subjects erred, simply to let them err, than that they should constrain them to lie and to say what is not in their hearts: neither is it right to defend evil with what is worse."

Protestants, because they champion religious liberty on a much larger basis than does the Declaration on Religious Freedom of the Second Vatican Council, in the main rejoice over its official adoption and promulgation, yet raise many questions not only in regard to the implementation of it, but also in respect to the whole matter of the nature of religious liberty itself and freedom of belief within the Church pertaining to doctrines and the interpretation of canon law.

Religious liberty, as most Protestants view it today, must include academic freedom as well as the right to freely express religious convictions within and without the Church, and without the penalties of censure (and censor) or excommunication.

The Declaration on Religious Freedom itself makes it very clear that it does not include these other basic freedoms. It clearly points out that the Declaration deals with conscience, with religious liberty, only as it pertains to the State or to the secular authority. It is emphatic in saying that it does not alter the dogma that the Roman Catholic

Church is the one true Church and that the members of the Roman Catholic Church are not permitted to think of all religious faiths as being of equal standing or worth. These matters of faith, which trouble both Protestants and Catholics, are yet to be dealt with officially by the theologians of the Church.

One of the best statements on religious liberty, from the Protestant viewpoint, is found in Report IV on the Church and the International Disorder of the first assembly of the World Council of Churches, Amsterdam, Holland, August 22 to September 4, 1948. After noting that "an essential element in a good international order is freedom of religion," and that "the rights of religious freedom herein declared shall be recognized and observed for all persons without distinction as to race, color, sex, language, or religion, and without imposition of disabilities by virtue of legal provision of administrative acts," it has several paragraphs of supporting material under each of the following captions:

1. "Every person has the right to determine his own faith and creed."

2. "Every person has the right to express his religious beliefs in worship, teaching and practice, and to proclaim the implications of his beliefs for relationships in a social and political community."

3. "Every person has the right to associate with others and to organize with them for religious purposes."

4. "Every religious organization, formed or maintained by action in accordance with the rights of individual persons, has the right to determine its policies and practices for the accomplishment of its chosen purposes."

A key paragraph, which indicates that Protestants and Orthodox had taken substantial action on religious liberty several years in advance of the Second Vatican Council, is this one:

"The rights which are claimed for the individual in his exercise of religious liberty become the rights of the religious organization, including the right to determine its faith and creed; to engage in religious worship, both public and private; to teach, educate, preach, and persuade; to express implications of belief for society and government. To these will be added certain corporate rights which derive from the rights

of individual persons, such as the right: to determine
the form of organization, its government, and conditions to membership; to select and train its own offi-
cers, leaders, and workers; to publish and circulate
religious literature; to carry on service and missionary
activities at home and abroad; to hold property and
to collect funds; to cooperate and to unite with other
religious bodies at home and in other lands, including freedom to invite or to send personnel beyond
national frontiers and to give or to receive financial
assistance; to use such facilities, open to all citizens or
associations, as will make possible the accomplishment of religious ends."

Naturally the real test in regard to religious freedom
is not in so many words on paper, but in the actual implementation of the principles stated. Nevertheless, the
statements are in a real sense action and now that the
Roman Catholic Church has joined those of other religious
faiths in principle, the common action should be much
easier. But in regard to this, particularly in certain areas of
State-Church arrangements, action is still in the future.

Since the Declaration on Religious Freedom is of such
a collateral nature to the Decree on Ecumenism, the question naturally arises, Why was it so long in being adopted?
Why was it postponed and revised so many times? Was
it because some of the bishops were afraid that such a
document would be misunderstood by the faithful and
therefore lead to indifferentism? Perhaps no one person
will know all the reasons for the delays and frustrations,
because in reality they may be a combination of many
considerations, some visible and others hidden. Probably
most will agree that by waiting we all got a better document, a document which is the companion to the splendid
Decree on Ecumenism. From the authors' point of view,
these two documents, taken together, represent a new birth
of freedom within the Roman Catholic Church which, in
turn, has created a new phase of the ecumenical movement.
Now the Anti-Reformation is over; the new era of Reform
and Renewal for the whole Church (Catholic, Protestant,
and Orthodox) has just begun.

Although internal freedom, that is freedom within the
Church itself, is not dealt with specifically in the Decree

on Religious Freedom, this does not mean that the Roman Catholic Church has not become much more free because of Vatican II. The very nature of the Council, with its open windows and frank discussion and development of doctrine, is now reflected in local parishes. Moreover, such documents as the Dogmatic Constitution on the Liturgy and the Decree on Ecumenism have given both clergy and laity much greater freedom within the Church. And the Pastoral Constitution on the Church in the Modern World has certainly opened up new areas for freedom of action. Taken as a whole, the accumulative result of Vatican II has given more freedom than the "average" priest or layman is apparently ready to employ.

While Protestants are pleased with the Declaration on Religious Freedom, many of them feel that it does not go anywhere near far enough. It is only a good beginning. Now, in this post-conciliar period, the real test will be its implementation in areas such as Spain,[1] Colombia in South America, and Los Angeles in the United States of America. Moreover, Protestants grow fearful when priests and theological students are denied freedom to support freely such causes as racial justice and world peace. Also, the whole area of academic freedom, especially in institutions of higher learning, raises many questions today. Protestants are not content just to protect a free conscience within the State; they firmly believe that in the modern world the Church will have to allow, and protect, and even promote, a free conscience within the Church itself.

Because religious freedom is directly related to mixed marriage, concordats with governments, and federal aid to parochial schools, besides the whole issue of liberty of conscience within the Church itself, this Declaration on Religious Freedom must be thought of as a point of be-

---

[1] The new Organic Law (Spanish Constitution) presented by General Franco on November 22, 1966 offers a measure of religious freedom to non-Catholics, but does not grant full religious liberty. According to the *St. Louis (Catholic) Review* of December 2, 1966:

"The new Organic Law, announced by General Franco, does nothing to change Spain's status vis-a-vis the Vatican as defined in the Concordat of Aug. 27, 1953, or to separate church and state.

"Spain's present laws say that Spain is a Catholic State and that 'the Spanish nation considers it a rule of honor to respect the law of God according to the doctrine of the Holy Apostolic Roman Church, the sole depository of truth.'"

ginning and not as the end. A great deal still needs to be done in order to set the conscience free. Another beginning has been made—with the abolition of the *Index* of forbidden books. Excommunications, for various reasons, are much more infrequent. But there is still much to be done.


## III. QUESTIONS FOR DISCUSSION

1. Why have Christians been so intolerant?

2. Does "error" have religious as well as civil rights?

3. At the present moment, where does the Roman Catholic Church (compared with the World Council of Churches) stand in relation to religious liberty?

4. Is there more academic freedom in Protestant colleges than in Catholic colleges?

5. How do the dogmas of the Church restrict religious freedom?

6. Is it necessary to have complete separation of Church and State in order to have full religious liberty?

7. To what extent does the Roman Catholic Church have more internal freedom than before the Second Vatican Council?

8. What progress has been made in religious freedom since Vatican II (due specifically to the Council)?

9. How much religious freedom does the new 1966 Constitution of Spain grant to non-Catholics?

10. In what way does the Concordat between the Vatican and Spain stand in the way of real religious freedom in Spain?


## IV. SUGGESTIONS FOR ECUMENICAL ACTION

1. Read the full text of the Declaration on Religious Freedom as found in *The Documents of Vatican II*.

2. Talk with a Protestant friend (with a Catholic if you are a Protestant) about how the Declaration on Religious Freedom should be implemented.

3. Read the 1948 Declaration of Human Rights of the United Nations. (See Appendix I.)

4. Discuss with a minister or priest the actions taken by the World Council of Churches on religious liberty.

5. Discover how the Declaration on Religious Freedom has changed conditions in Spain, South America, and the town in which you live.

"We cannot in truthfulness call upon that God who is the Father of all if we refuse to act in a brotherly way toward certain men, created though they be to God's image. A man's relationship with God the Father and his relationship with his brother men are so linked together that Scripture says: 'He who does not love does not know God' (1 Jn. 4:8)." (Declaration on the Relation of the Church to Non-Christian Religions, Art. 5.)

CHAPTER XI

# The Jews and Other Non-Christians

## INTRODUCTION

The Jews for us "are not objects of reprobation or distrust, but of respect, love and hope."—Pope Paul VI, Oct. 28, 1965, promulgating the Declaration on the Relation of the Church to Non-Christian Religions *(Nostra Aetate)*.

Among the seven major actions of the Second Vatican Council: "Condemnation of anti-Semitism in an unequivocal manner."—Dr. Albert Outler, *Protestant Observer.*

"Approved with all essentials intact."—National Council of Churches, *Faith and Order Trends,* Dec. 1965.

May come to be regarded "as the great achievement of Vatican II."—"It rejects all forms of anti-Semitism, it exhorts all teachers of the Christian gospel to be faithful to the truth, it encourages dialogue and cooperation between Christians and Jews. More than that, it acknowledges the common spiritual patrimony between the Church and the Synagogue."—Fr. Gregory Baum, O.S.A., in *Commonweal,* Nov. 26, 1965.

". . . the occasion for renewed query about ourselves as Christians . . . Never before has the Church gone so formally on record in affirming the positive elements in ancient and contemporary non-Christian religiosity. . . ."— Dr. George H. Williams, *Protestant observer* on panel at Interchurch Center, Jan. 1966.

". . . constitutes a clean break with the Middle Ages. . . ."—Fr. John B. Sheerin, C.S.P., Council "expert" on panel at Interchurch Center, Jan. 1966.

"The monstrous crimes of Nazi anti-Semitism would have been impossible without the hidden and, often enough, open 'Christian' anti-Semitism of more than 1,500 years, an anti-Semitism which was manifest even in the Council debates."—Fr. Hans Küng, Council "expert," *Commonweal*, Jan. 21, 1966.

Note will be taken later of statements in the Declaration concerning non-Jewish religions, but precedence is given to those on relations with the Jewish religion since those relations are currently the most difficult and important for both the Vatican Council and the World Council of Churches, most relevant to continuing discrimination and persecutions, and of most immediate interest to Americans of all faiths or none—and the most controverted and criticized.

# I. THE NEW ROMAN CATHOLIC POSITION

"In our times, when every day men are being drawn closer together and the ties between various peoples are being multiplied, the Church is giving deeper study to her relationship with non-Christian religions. In her task of fostering unity and love among men, and even among nations, she gives primary consideration in this document to what human beings have in common and to what promotes fellowship among them." (Art. 1.)

Here, and for the first time in history, an ancient and self-sufficient Church (sufficient, of course, in dependence on God) undertakes to evaluate other religions, in summary but searching fashion, and describe its relation to each, as seen from its side. Not exhaustive from its side, nor satisfying from their side, but an honest if awkward preamble to dialogue, and a momentous cultural-religious event.

This introductory paragraph is followed by the recognition of the community of all peoples and the common questions of all religions, and the acknowledgment of "that ultimate and unutterable mystery which engulfs our being, and whence we take our rise, and whither our journey leads us." (Art. 1.)

> "As this sacred Synod searches into the mystery of the Church, it recalls the spiritual bond linking the people of the New Covenant with Abraham's stock.
>
> "For the Church of Christ acknowledges that, according to the mystery of God's saving design, the beginnings of her faith and her election are already found among the patriarchs, Moses, and the prophets. She professes that all who believe in Christ, Abraham's sons according to faith (cf. Gal. 3:7), are included in the same patriarch's call, and likewise that the salvation of the Church was mystically foreshadowed by the chosen people's exodus from the land of bondage.
>
> "The Church, therefore, cannot forget that she received the revelation of the Old Testament through the people with whom God in His inexpressible mercy deigned to establish the Ancient Covenant. Nor can she forget that she draws sustenance from the root of that good olive tree into which have been grafted the wild olive branches of the Gentiles (cf. Rom. 11:17-24). Indeed, the Church believes that by His cross Christ, our Peace, reconciled Jew and Gentile, making them both one in Himself (cf. Eph. 2:14-16)." (Art. 4.)

The debt to the Covenant religion of the pre-Christian era is expressed clearly and cordially. If one looks for an implication of condescension in these paragraphs, it must be sought in the absence of any such approach to dialogue with members of the Jewish religion of today, or foundation for it, as is to be found in the eighteen lines addressed to Moslems.

The debt, if remembered, is too great to leave any room for disdain, let alone persecution. The gap is being rapidly filled by dialogues, institutes, and intervisitation between church and synagogue.

Nevertheless, if the reconciliation of the cross is to be realized within history, more direct bridge building between gospel and Torah at Vatican or papal level would seem to be desirable, the sooner the better. Obstacles are found in the New Testament itself, as indicated in the following paragraphs:

"Also, the Church ever keeps in mind the words of the Apostle about his kinsmen, 'who have the adoption as sons, and the glory and the covenant and the legislation and the worship and the promises; who have the fathers, and from whom is Christ according to the flesh' (Rom. 9:4-5), the son of the Virgin Mary. The Church recalls too that from the Jewish people sprang the apostles, her foundation stones and pillars, as well as most of the early disciples who proclaimed Christ to the world.

"As holy Scripture testifies, Jerusalem did not recognize the time of her visitation (cf. Lk. 19:44), nor did the Jews in large number accept the gospel; indeed, not a few opposed the spreading of it (cf. Rom. 11:28). Nevertheless, according to the Apostle, the Jews still remain most dear to God because of their fathers, for He does not repent of the gifts He makes nor of the calls He issues (cf. Rom. 11:28-29). In company with the prophets and the same Apostle, the Church awaits that day, known to God alone, on which all peoples will address the Lord in a single voice and 'serve him with one accord' (Soph. 3:9; cf. Is. 66:23; Ps. 65:4; Rom. 11:11-32)." (Art. 4.)

The concluding four paragraphs of Art. 4 come closer to the present situation:

"Since the spiritual patrimony common to Christians and Jews is thus so great, this sacred Synod wishes to foster and recommend that mutual understanding and respect which is the fruit above all of biblical and theological studies, and of brotherly dialogues.

"True, authorities of the Jews and those who followed their lead pressed for the death of Christ (cf. Jn. 19:6); still, what happened in His passion cannot be blamed upon all the Jews then living, without distinction, nor upon the Jews of today. Although the

Church is the new People of God, the Jews should not be presented as repudiated or cursed by God, as if such views followed from the holy Scriptures. All should take pains, then, lest in catechetical instruction and in the preaching of God's word they teach anything out of harmony with the truth of the gospel and the spirit of Christ.

"The Church repudiates all persecutions against any man. Moreover, mindful of her common patrimony with the Jews, and motivated by the gospel's spiritual love and by no political considerations, she deplores the hatred, persecutions, and displays of anti-Semitism directed against the Jews at any time and from any source.

"Besides, as the Church has always held and continues to hold, Christ in His boundless love freely underwent His passion and death because of the sins of all men, so that all might attain salvation. It is, therefore, the duty of the Church's preaching to proclaim the cross of Christ as the sign of God's all-embracing love and as the fountain from which every grace flows."

An attempt is made to counteract a traditional interpretation, "as if such views followed from the holy Scriptures." Much reinterpretation will be needed here—not only dialogue and fresh exegesis, but a weighing of isolated texts in the light of the whole gospel, of St. Paul's agony, of Jesus' own spirit. The injunction to Catholic teachers and preachers is forthright—but they will need help.

Forthright, also, is the repudiation of "every persecution" —henceforth! What about past guilt? Comment is reserved till later, for both World Council and Vatican Council.

From the Christian side, the cross of Christ is adequate for reconciliation. Is there to be no search from the Christian side for that in the modern Jewish religion which can replace Christian monologue with Christian-Jewish dialogue? The Christian *must* preach the cross of Christ. But he cannot assume or insist upon its acceptance as the basis of dialogue. For centuries Christians have put Jews on the cross; some degree of Christian repentance is required. If his clear and necessary witness is confused in his Jewish neighbor's mind with an intended proselytism, dialogue and effective preaching are alike inhibited. The impact of the truth depends upon the work of the Holy Spirit; Christians should therefore listen also to the truth that can come to them through the Jews.

**OTHER RELIGIONS.** There are some thirteen million Jews in the world, ethnically reckoned, many fewer religiously speaking. Their importance for Christians is indicated by the New Testament statement that "salvation is of the Jews" and by Pope Pius XII's affirmation that "we are all Semites."

But for the broadest religious ecumenism, and for goodwill among men as the foundation of world peace—and certainly in the long sweep of history—relations with the hundreds of millions of Mohammedans, Buddhists, and Hindus are of incalculable importance. Consider only two implications, for the moment, of the following passages from the Declaration—for the Christian mission, and for world peace, particularly in the light of the vote by the National Inter-Religious Peace Conference, Washington, D. C., March 1966, calling for a peace conference of all nations and all religions.

"Thus in Hinduism men contemplate the divine mystery and express it through an unspent fruitfulness of myths and through searching philosophical inquiry. They seek release from the anguish of our condition through ascetical practices or deep meditation or a loving, trusting flight toward God.

"Buddhism in its multiple forms acknowledges the radical insufficiency of this shifting world. It teaches a path by which men, in a devout and confident spirit, can either reach a state of absolute freedom or attain supreme enlightenment by their own efforts or by higher assistance.

"The Catholic Church rejects nothing which is true and holy in these religions. . . .

"The Church therefore has this exhortation for her sons: prudently and lovingly, through dialogue and collaboration with the followers of other religions, and in witness of Christian faith and life, acknowledge, preserve, and promote the spiritual and moral goods found among these men, as well as the values in their society and culture." (Art. 2.)

"Upon the Moslems, too, the Church looks with

esteem. They adore one God, living and enduring, merciful and all-powerful, Maker of heaven and earth and Speaker to men. They strive to submit whole-heartedly even to His inscrutable decrees, just as did Abraham, with whom the Islamic faith is pleased to associate itself. Though they do not acknowledge Jesus as God, they revere Him as a prophet. They also honor Mary, His virgin mother; at times they call on her, too, with devotion. In addition they await the day of judgment when God will give each man his due after raising him up. Consequently, they prize the moral life, and give worship to God especially through prayer, almsgiving, and fasting.

"Although in the course of the centuries many quarrels and hostilities have arisen between Christians and Moslems, this most sacred Synod urges all to forget the past and to strive sincerely for mutual understanding. On behalf of all mankind, let them make common cause of safeguarding and fostering social justice, moral values, peace, and freedom." (Art. 3.)

Obviously, none of the statements relating to the four religions is offered as a theological, historical, or cultural basis for bilateral or multilateral dialogue. Both Christians and non-Christians will have varying views as to their adequacy, in attitude and spirit, as invitations or preambles to dialogue. But the intention can scarcely be doubted.

For the intention coincides with that of the Pastoral Constitution on the Church in the Modern World. No longer threats, anathemas, defense against all that is not Roman Catholic. The weather shows signs of changing from cold and windy to warm and sunny.

## II. CORRESPONDING PROTESTANT AND ORTHODOX POSITIONS

**A. HISTORICAL SHARING OF GUILT.** The uniform pattern in the "Christian" countries of Europe has been segregation or expulsion of Jews until modern times, when some relaxation and some relapses have occurred. Symptomatic was the Dreyfus case in France, with a horrible parallel, less well known, in Atlanta's Frank case. Russia perpetrated pogroms and still discriminates. Christian involvement in Hitler's attempted genocide is attested in the quotation from Hans Küng. We cannot yet say of any locality that the attitude of a Christian majority of the community ("community"?) guarantees Jewish citizens against both major and minor forms of persecution, discrimination, annoyance.

Both the World Council of Churches (discussing the matter at Evanston and at New Delhi) and the Second Vatican Council adopted forthright declarations condemning anti-Semitic interpretations of Christianity and abjuring future discrimination. These declarations are a new starting point for the removal of remaining abuses and the development of a brotherly spirit and practices between Christians and Jews.

But while in both assemblies many, probably most, had a deep sense of guilt, they produced no satisfying confession of guilt. Three possible reasons for this are worth considering. No confession, so soon after the gas-chamber massacres, and with no possible material reparation or spiritual atonement conceivable, could satisfy either Christians or Jews. Also, there would have been more than a suggestion of confessing the sins of other persons, other lands, bygone generations. There was, in addition, the lack of such theological preparation and agreement as would have permitted the repudiation of the conduct of Christians without the seeming repudiation of some biblical texts and much of the Christian catechism and liturgy. The third was probably operative; none of the three may have played an important conscious role. We turn to a difference between Rome and New Delhi.

**B. AN INTERESTING DIFFERENCE IN THE NON-CATHOLIC DELIBERATIONS.** At New Delhi, there were representatives of lands and cultures that had not been characterized by anti-Semitism, and they were ecclesiastically independent, not deeply involved in the denominational or confessional guilt of the past, but only in the general historical Christian responsibility. Protestant leaders from the West prevailed upon them to permit the passage of a condemnation of anti-Semitism for the future, without accepting theological responsibility for the past.

At Vatican II, of course, all were voting as Catholics in communion with the Bishop of Rome. Opposition there was, tenacious and hurtful. Much of it came from the churches of the Near East, and was compounded of ancient doctrine and contemporary politics.

The anti-Semitic doctrine propounded by post-Apostolic Fathers of the Church, particularly the otherwise great St. John Chrysostom, had not been repudiated or modified by any authoritative body, and could have been cited reputably as Christian in all three confessions. Christians in the Near East adhered to it actively.

Many of them, living among Arabs, feared the effects of adopting a declaration that might increase the political weight of Israel. The Arab opposition to the Declaration decreased notably from the third session, 1964, to the fourth session; misrepresentation and suppression of the true text gave way to more reasonable opposition. It was still thought necessary not only to disclaim political intentions in the public defense of the text, but also in the declaration itself to assert that the Church was moved not by "political considerations" but by "the gospel's spiritual love."

The opposition in the Vatican Council was more embarrassing than that in the World Council. The attempt to purge the Jews of the charge of "deicide" was frustrating and frustrated. Had the word never been included, the statement would not have been weakened. In fact, the term deicide had been exposed by the Catechism of Trent as a theologically false term. Just how anyone could kill God is not easy to explain. And Jews could not have intended deicide, since they could not consider Jesus as God without blasphemy.

In the same sentence as the disclaimer of political considerations was at one time a condemnation of "hatred, persecutions, displays of anti-Semitism directed against Jews at any time and from any source." But the word "condemns" was criticized as being traditionally reserved for specific ecclesiastical anathema (rather lamely some felt) and was replaced in the English text first by "decries" and later by "deplores." The strength of the passage will depend in any case on the vigor and sincerity with which clergy and laity reform catechism, liturgy, preaching, and conduct—just as is the case with Orthodox and Protestants.

## III. QUESTIONS FOR DISCUSSION

1. Is there any marked difference between the texts of the New Delhi and Vatican II declarations on the Jews?

2. Why has the New Delhi statement attracted so much less attention?

3. On what basis can Christians seek to evangelize Jews?

4. Why do not Jews seek to proselytize?

5. What do you think of the historic separation of Church and Synagogue as "schism" or "proto-schism"?

6. Can Jews be "saved"?

7. How can Jews become a part of the ecumenical movement?

8. What do Christians inherit from the Jews?

9. At what points can Christians and Jews have full cooperation?


## IV. SUGGESTIONS FOR ECUMENICAL ACTION

1. Study the text of the Declaration on the Relationship of the Church to Non-Christian Religions found in *The Documents of Vatican II*.

2. Compare the texts of the New Delhi and Vatican II declarations.

3. Note the differences between witness and proselytism.

4. Compare the implications of "conversion" as applied by Christians to Jews with those of "return," as applied by Roman Catholics to Protestants.

5. Visit a synagogue.

6. Talk with a rabbi concerning his religious faith.

"From the very infancy of the Church, there have existed men and women who strove to follow Christ more freely and imitate Him more nearly by the practice of the evangelical counsels." (Decree on the Appropriate Renewal of the Religious Life, Art. 1.)

## CHAPTER XII

# Reform and Renewal

## INTRODUCTION

Judging by Pope John's words and decisions at critical points, and by the acts of the Council as a whole, we can consider Vatican II to have been the Council of Reform and Renewal. Three Vatican II Decrees—on Eastern Catholic Churches, on the Appropriate Renewal of the Religious Life, and on the Bishops' Pastoral Office in the Church—are included in the chapter under this heading— Reform and Renewal. The brief comments below will explain why.

A great ecumenical question is whether the Eastern Churches which are in allegiance to Rome shall continue to be a barrier in the way of Eastern Orthodox reunion with the Latin Church, or become a bridge. In any case, those six churches themselves had felt at some points more like adopted children, or orphans, than full members of the papal household. The Decree on the Eastern Catholic Churches (*Orientalum Ecclesiarum*) was promulgated by Pope Paul VI on November 21, 1964.

Attention had to be given to the appropriate renewal of the religious life for the sake of the religious orders themselves, and to fit them better for their role in the mission of the whole Church, i.e., as a part of the pronounced pastoral orientation of the Council as a whole. Their role in the Church involves their relations with the bishops. The Decree on the Appropriate Renewal of the Religious Life *(Perfectae Caritatis)* was promulgated by Pope Paul VI on October 28, 1965.

The Bishops' pastoral office in the Church cannot be separated from their newly confirmed role as successors of the apostles, the great emphasis on their responsibility to teach, and the potential bearing of both these factors on the doctrine of papal infallibility, perhaps still more on its practice, and—in the long run—on its image. The Document on the Bishops' Pastoral Office *(Christus Dominus)* was also promulgated by Pope Paul VI on October 28, 1965.

## I. THE THREE DECREES

> **DECREE ON EASTERN CATHOLIC CHURCHES.** "History, tradition, and numerous ecclesiastical institutions manifest luminously how much the universal Church is indebted to the Eastern Churches. This sacred Synod, therefore, not only honors this ecclesiastical and spiritual heritage with merited esteem and rightful praise, but also unhesitatingly looks upon it as the heritage of Christ's universal Church." (Art. 5.)

The Decree praises variety among the churches, provided they have the same faith, the same sacraments, the same hierarchical government, and are "equally entrusted to the pastoral guidance of the Roman Pontiff, the divinely appointed successor of St. Peter." (Art. 3.)

In the Near East, jurisdictions in affiliation with Rome overlap territorially. Bishops of the different rites, all of the same dignity, are enjoined to cooperate for the necessary degree of uniformity, and for unity of action. There are six Eastern Patriarchs involved: the Coptic Patriarch of Alexandria; the Melkite Patriarch of Antioch, whose title includes Alexandria and Jerusalem; the Syrian and Maronite Patriarchs, who have the title of Antioch; the Armenian and Chaldean Patriarchs. (Ruthenians and Ukrainians are not covered in this Decree.) In the case of marriages between persons of two of these rites, the earlier rule still holds in North America: the rites of the bride-groom determines both the choice of the priest and the rearing of the children.

The Decree does not treat of the question of the comparative rank and role of patriarchs and cardinals. Well after Vatican II was under way, the patriarchs in the Council were seated nearly opposite the cardinals, perhaps more as a courtesy than as a legal act. The outspoken Patriarch Maximos of Antioch (Melkite) said more than once that he would not accept a cardinal's hat, but finally did so. Since historically the creation of patriarchs far antedates that of cardinals, since patriarchs can claim to belong to the whole historic Church, since they do not vote in the election of the Pope, the Eastern churches can hardly be satisfied with this Decree. It specifies that the patriarch has jurisdiction over all members and clergy of his rite, including metropolitans, even those functioning outside the home territory of the patriarch. One recalls that the cardinal residing in Venice is also a patriarch, in the Latin rite.

The right of priests of one rite to confirm candidates of another was upheld (in some cases restored) by the Decree. This applies reciprocally, of course, and includes those of the Latin rite; it is without prejudice to the candidate's allegiance. These provisions apply where the rites overlap territorially.

The Decree recommends that the office of the permanent deacon be restored—more for liturgical than for pastoral help, it is reported. Pilus XII in *Cleri sanctitate* had prescribed the discipline of celibacy for subdeacons as for higher orders; the Decree restores the ancient rights and obligations, according to the decisions of "each individual church." In mixed territories, priests of one rite may hear the confessions of members of another rite, unless their bishop expressly forbids it. The Decree relaxes somewhat the requirements for the validity (not the legality) of marriages involving persons of different rites.

Uniformity of the dates of Easter and other feast days, determined by agreement between authorities of the various rites in a territory, is recommended. Those authorities may also determine the language to be used in the liturgy. With Rome's permission, translations into the vernacular may be made and used.

In the section on relations with the brethren of separated

churches (Arts. 24-29) the Decree refers to the Decree on Ecumenism. The commentator on this Decree in the post-conciliar semi-official special edition of *Osservatore della Domenica* calls attention to the fact that the two Decrees (Eastern Churches and Ecumenism) and the Dogmatic Constitution on the Church were in fact promulgated simultaneously at the end of the third session. For him, they constitute an indivisible trilogy.

The Decree provides that members and priests may pass from the Eastern Orthodox to the Roman Catholic faith without rebaptism or reordination: the validity of their faith and orders, respectively, is not in question. The priest would be subject to the same rules as other Catholic priests in the exercise of his functions.

Articles 26-29 provide certain relaxations with regard to common worship *(communicatio in sacris)* for Eastern Orthodox who find it desirable to join with Roman Catholics and vice versa. This can be of especial importance in the totalitarian territories where thousands have no access to a priest of their own rite, and in Moslem territories where Christians sometimes constitute a very small fraction of the population.

The Decree concludes with an expression of joy in the "fruitful and zealous collaboration between the Eastern and the Western Catholic churches," admittedly incomplete, and calls for prayer and love to increase their unity.

While it is evident that the Eastern Churches can not be satisfied with the treatment of the patriarchs in the Decree, they voted for the Decree as a promising development. Much is left to be worked out by various Synods, in consultation with Rome. Also, completion can scarcely be realized until the Eastern Orthodox and Roman Catholics find themselves in unity, with some form of union or genuine interconfessional harmony and cooperation. Rome has perhaps taken rather a long step in this Decree in recognizing unity in diversity, not merely tolerating a certain degree of diversity under the aegis of canonical unity. But Rome has yet to abandon the attempt to legislate for the East in Western terms: real dialogue has not begun, so far as one can judge from matters of public knowledge. Taken with the Constitutions on the Church and the Decree on Ecumenism, this Decree is an example of Rome's earnest desire for sincere conversation with all the Eastern Churches on a basis of equality.

**DECREE ON THE APPROPRIATE RENEWAL OF THE RELIGIOUS LIFE.** "Therefore, in fidelity to their profession and in renunciation of all things for the sake of Christ, let religious follow Him as their one necessity. Let them listen to His words and be preoccupied with His work . . . combine contemplation with apostolic love . . . adhere to God in mind and heart . . . strive to associate themselves with the work of redemption and to spread the Kingdom of God." (Art. 5.)

The above indicates the tone and theological atmosphere of this Decree. Fuller theological grounding is provided, in the five articles on "religious" in Chapter VI of the Dogmatic Constitution on the Church. This arrangement was by agreement between the two Commissions that prepared the two Schemata for submission to the Council. Both the Constitution and the Decree refer to the variety of the communities or orders, and to their value to the Church.

The Decree lays down general principles, leaving to the communities themselves—guided and permitted by the Holy See—to modernize their rules, programs, and habits, and to bring all into harmony with the acts of the Second Vatican Council.

Internal, spiritual renewal, and adaptation to the needs of today's world are objectives of the Decree. Renewal of the religious life, it says, involves constantly and simultaneously, 1) a return to the sources of all religious life and to the original inspiration of the order's founder, and 2) an adjustment to changing times—involving both close participation in the life of the whole Church, and constant imitation of Christ. *Aggiornamento* within the community is spelled out, all items involved being mentioned—physical and psychological conditions, the surrounding culture, its own rules, "custom books" (handbooks), directories, prayers, and ceremonies. This requires the suppression of outmoded regulations. Some orders initiated the call for the tasks of renewal and coordination with Vatican II before the Council adjourned.

Communities and their members totally dedicated to contemplation are not out-of-date, but serve the Church with "the richest splendors of sanctity"; "they are the glory of the Church and an overflowing fountain of heavenly graces." (Art. 7.) Other nuns in orders "devoted to external works" (Art. 16) determine the character and degree of their cloister rules; the contemplative ones have papally sanctioned rules for their cloisters.

The Council expressed esteem for the monastic life in general, East and West, and for the lay religious life, both for men and for women. Lay brothers may be admitted to holy orders for service to their own chapter, provided the character of the community be not changed.

The three vows—chastity, poverty, and obedience—are justified in the Decree. Complete continence need not be harmful; it is easier in a community of fraternal love. Voluntary poverty enables one to share in the poverty of Christ. Obedience is the sacrifice of the will to God; the superiors should also be "docile to God's will" (Art. 14) in dealing with those under their care.

The garb of the religious "should be simple and modest, at once poor and becoming." (Art. 17.) Changes were being considered and requested before the Decree was finished.

Novices require thorough training, beyond the novitiate, before being assigned to apostolic works. "Apostolic" takes on added significance when the Decree speaks of the primitive Church as being "of one heart and one mind" (Art. 15), a fitting example for the communities. However, they must be acquainted with "the prevailing manners of contemporary social life" and "its characteristic ways of feeling and thinking." (Art. 18.) This is especially true in occupying new territory, where new forms of religious life may have to be devised to fit the needs of native customs and character, as well as those of the universal Church.

If the Holy See and the appropriate bishops see no "reasonable hope of flourishing" (Art. 21) any longer, they may order a given community not to receive any more novices.

Cooperation or union among kindred "independent communities and monasteries" (Art. 22) is advised. Major superiors should form conferences or councils to widen the vision of the communities, and to coordinate their external works.

The Church declares its high regard and "steady hope," and calls the religious to faithful witness of the "good news of Christ." (Art. 25.)

**DECREE ON THE BISHOPS' PASTORAL OFFICE IN THE CHURCH.** "Christ gave the apostles and their successors the command and the power to teach all nations, to hallow men in the truth, and to feed them. Hence, through the Holy Spirit who has been given to them, bishops have been made true and authentic teachers of the faith, pontiffs, and shepherds." (Art. 2.)

The above quotation links this Decree with Chapter III of the Dogmatic Constitution on the Church. We have collected our comment in these introductory paragraphs rather than scatter it through the references to the various articles of the Decree. Students will find it enriching to read the comments of Archbishop Hallinan and the response of Bishop Corson to the Decree in *The Documents of Vatican II.*

It was not until September 1965 that the bishops saw this Decree in its approximately final form, but they finished discussion and revision in time for it to be finally voted on and promulgated, October 28.

Together, the Constitution and the Decree confirm that bishops are successors of the apostles—not merely delegated appointees of the Pope; that with the Pope, collegially, they constitute the highest spiritual and teaching authority of the Church. The Pope's authority when acting alone is not thereby constitutionally diminished—but the need, the occasion, and the appropriateness of his acting alone "infallibly" is greatly reduced.

The Council itself was a superb example of collegiality. The institution of a representative Synod of bishops to be called together to inform and advise the Pontiff when the Council is not in session makes it possible for "infallibility" to be exercised by the Church as a whole, under the guidance of the Holy Spirit. The collegial principle also makes it possible to restrict a reformed Curia to administrative duties on behalf of Pope *and* bishops, almost eliminating the function of the Curia as a link between bishops and Pope, either as bridge or barrier.

Regional conferences of bishops may now continue their development with renewed confidence, and may address the Pope with assurance.

The ecumenical effects of the new or renewed image and role of the Roman bishops may be considerable. As it diminishes the fear of the hurtful exercise of papal infallibility and the sometimes reactionary influence of the Curia, it is to be welcomed. A bishop's own figure can be enhanced if he is diligent in extending the principle and the spirit of collegiality to the clergy and laity in his diocese and to his colleagues around the world—he is a bishop not merely of a diocese but of the whole Church.

One cannot be sure of what the temporary effect of the new image of the bishop will be on those Protestants who are seeking unity and looking ahead toward union some day, but who do not have bishops—certainly not bishops with the image that Vatican II wishes Rome's bishops to earn.

The Preface to the Decree not only reaffirms the charismatic character of the bishop, but states briefly the doctrine of collegiality, and of responsibility in and for the whole Church.

Chapter I, the Relationship of Bishops to the Universal Church, confirms in Articles 4-7 the role of the bishop in the universal Church, and spells out some of the practical details: financial and other assistance to new or weak areas and to sister dioceses in times of disaster or other emergency, and support for bishops who are harassed or persecuted.

Articles 8-10 confirm that the bishop has full authority in his diocese except as the Pope may reserve certain matters for decision by the Holy See. Since the adjournment of Vatican II, Pope Paul has somewhat reduced the number of matters thus reserved. The Council asked that the Curia be reorganized and better adapted to present needs, and that "the office of legates of the Roman Pontiff be more precisely determined." The Curia, it said, should be made more representative by drawing its members from a greater variety of geographical areas and by adding diocesan bishops. The bishops suggested that laymen should be heard by Curial departments (other Vatican II documents also enjoin the bishops to hear laymen).

"A diocese is that portion of God's people which is entrusted to a bishop to be shepherded by him with the cooperation of the presbytery." (Ch. II, Art. 11.) Articles 12-14 emphasize the bishop's role as teacher, not only proclaiming the doctrine and formulated message of the Church—to unbelievers as well as believers—but also showing their relevance to the needs of men, very much in the same areas of modern life and problems as are indicated in the Pastoral Constitution on the Church in the Modern World. He must take care to provide properly trained catechists and see that children, as well as youth and adults, are given proper instruction. The bishop should use modern methods of communication "to proclaim the gospel of Christ." (Art. 13.)

"As those who lead others to perfection, bishops should be diligent in fostering holiness among their clerics, religious, and laity according to the special vocation of each. They should also be mindful of their obligation to give an example of holiness through charity, humility, and simplicity of life." (Art. 15.) Only with such an assumption could the Constitution on the Sacred Liturgy speak of the bishop as "the high priest of his flock," . . . from whom "the faithful who are under his care derive and maintain their life in Christ."

The bishop must be shepherd, father, trainer, concerned with the "spiritual, intellectual, and material condition of his priests," encouraging institutes and research to ground them in the knowledge and skills required for an effective pastorate. The bishop "should deal lovingly with the separated brethren." (Art. 16).

Laymen should be involved in some of the infinitely varied ministries. Care should be taken to provide a ministry to migrants, including servants of the government, and to shut-ins. Some ministries involve planning and cooperation by the conference of bishops in the territory involved. As ministers, they are independent of civil authorities; they should cooperate in efforts toward civic progress. To maintain due independence, the Church "desires that in the future no rights or privileges of election, nomination, presentation, or designation for the office of bishop be any longer granted to civil authorities." (Art. 20.) In Article 21, provision is made for the retirement and support of bishops too infirm for continued activity. The same provision is made for priests, later in the Decree.

Three articles, 22-24, largely technical, deal with diocesan boundaries—unity, size, and early correction of existing misfits. Articles 25-26 deal with coadjutor and auxiliary bishops, and Article 27 with the diocesan curia and councils. For the non-Catholic, these articles are largely technical, but they give ample scope for collegial practices within the diocese. New terms are "episcopal vicars," with authority in part of the diocese; and "pastoral commission," a selected group to aid in pastoral decisions.

Articles 28-32 deal with the diocesan clergy and the cure of souls. Most directly involved here are the parish priests, who should be closely united with the bishop and with each other. The place of supraparochial ministers and of supervisors is recognized. Parish priests are to cultivate with their parishioners the sense of being truly a part of the Church; they must also be missionaries. To aid them in their catechetical work, they should involve "religious" and lay people, and should organize the Confraternity of Christian Doctrine. Effective use of the sacraments and the liturgy is enjoined, and the shepherd is advised to know his sheep by visitation, especially the ill, youth, and workingmen—enlisting all these in the apostolate. Priests are to be assigned according to their aptitude and ability in the performance of these manifold duties in the given parish.

Articles 33-35 deal with the external duties of the religious, the organization and internal life of their orders being dealt with in the Decree on the Appropriate Renewal of the Religious Life. Priests among the religious are to consider themselves part of the clergy of the diocese, since they share in the care of souls and in the apostolate. Conference and cooperation of superiors of orders with the bishop are recommended, in order that the vows and loyalties of religious to the order may not exclude needed and proper service in the diocese.

Chapter III deals with the cooperation of bishops for the common good of many churches. The venerable character of synods and councils is underscored; regional conferences have been developing in this century; all three are needed. An episcopal conference "is a kind of council" (Art. 38) for a given territory: six "decrees" are issued to govern them. "Local Ordinaries and coadjutors hold a deliberative vote" which the conference may extend to auxiliaries and others who have by right a consultative voice. The conference organizes and governs itself. Decisions by two-thirds vote, and sanctioned by the Apostolic See, are binding—this goes beyond cooperation by unanimous consent. Episcopal conferences of Oriental Churches should include all the rites in the territory. Several nations may be represented in an episcopal conference.

Three brief articles (39-41) provide for study and re-

vision of diocesan boundaries. Detached dioceses should
be attached to the most convenient ecclesiastical province
rather than left to depend directly on papal jurisdiction.
Bishops' conferences may assist in the reform of diocesan
boundaries. All revisions require Rome's sanction.

Interdiocesan authority and the military vicariate are
briefly treated in Articles 42 and 43.

Article 44 directs that the Decree as a whole is to be
kept in mind in revision of the Code of Canon Law,
manuals, directories, etc.

Taken as a whole, this Decree, in line with the over-all
spirit and tendency of Vatican II, moves from a juridical
toward a pastoral concept. It may be remarked that if the
episcopacy did not move in that direction much of the
pastoral intention of the Council and of Pope John would
prove illusory.

# II. AGREEMENTS AND DISAGREEMENTS

With regard to these three Decrees, many Protestants,
perhaps most, will raise the question of the Decrees'
relevance to their concerns, rather than of approval or
disapproval.

The Decree on Eastern Catholic Churches is of immediate relevance and concern for all the Patriarchates of the
Eastern Orthodox Churches, under the spiritual leadership
of Ecumenical Patriarch Athenagoras of Istanbul (the
traditional name of the beloved, almost holy capital, Constantinople, is still widely used by the Orthodox). They are
in the World Council of Churches and over forty years
ago the Ecumenical Patriarch of that period called for
Christian unity. Less authoritarian, less centralized, less
clerical than the Latin Church, they are close to it in
rites and doctrine. They also have strong ties with Anglicans. They may well prove to be in the most strategic
position in the ecumenical movement. If, as seems to be
true, they see in this Decree a small step toward reconciliation, that is important for the World and National
Councils of Churches, and for all who seek Christian
unity.

Of the Decree on the Appropriate Renewal of the
Religious Life, much the same observations hold true.
Religious orders are as much a traditional and con-

temporary feature of the East as of the Church of Rome. In the Anglican Church, there has been a revival of religious communities in the past century. There exist somewhat similar communities of denominationally mixed Protestant origin and membership, with little or no church affiliation; some of them are made up of families. Thus there is a rich variety of religious communities from which the whole People of God should draw inspiration and guidance.

The Decree on the Bishops' Pastoral Office in the Church is of wider relevance. Orthodox, Anglicans, European Lutherans, and most Methodists have bishops, and it would seemingly not be very difficult for Presbyterians to adopt an episcopal structure and polity.

Protestants must insist—as Catholics affirm but have not emphasized—that the congregation is, in essentials, the Church, *in parvo*. Borrowing a term from the Decree on Religious Freedom, they might say that the Church "subsists" in the local unit. Where can the Church be found, if not there?

However, both urban and ecumenical developments, in different ways, could transform the life of the local church in the decades just ahead. It cannot save itself, in most places, except by complete dedication to the effort to save the city. This is likely to involve increased denominational cooperation through councils and by merger.

## III. QUESTIONS FOR DISCUSSION

1. Why did the national Greek Church not send delegated observers to Vatican II?

2. Why are six Eastern Churches in communion with the Bishop of Rome rather than with the Patriarch of Constantinople?

3. What values, or disvalues, do you see, for church and individuals, in voluntary vows of permanent chastity, poverty, and obedience, dutifully observed?—in a celibate clergy?—in exclusively contemplative communities?

4. What has been the historic contribution of religious orders?

5. In view of the Christian mission in the world and to the world, what is the necessary teaching authority of the Church—local, denominational, conciliar, universal? How

is it related to the Bible? To tradition? To the individual conscience, intelligence, will? To the Holy Spirit?

6. What practical significance, if any, would you attach to a doctrine of the infallibility of the Church of Jesus Christ? How could such a doctrine be formulated or defined in order that it might have meaning?

7. These three Decrees discussed in Chapter XII cover a wide area of interest, and interlock with other pronouncements of Vatican II: what do you find in them, not suggested by comments and questions in this chapter?


# IV. SUGGESTIONS FOR ECUMENICAL ACTION

1. Read the following in *The Documents of Vatican II:* Decree on Eastern Catholic Churches, Decree on the Appropriate Renewal of the Religious Life, and the Decree on the Bishops' Pastoral Office in the Church.

2. Visit an Eastern Orthodox Church.

3. Compare the different functions and ecclesiastical status of Roman Catholic, Eastern Orthodox, and Protestant bishops.

4. Discover where bishops fit into the Consultation on Church Union.

5. Go to the dictionary and find the meaning of the word "hierarchy."

6. Find out why the Roman Catholic Church does not accept as valid the ordination of Anglican priests.

7. Study the structure of the new National Conference of Catholic Bishops.

EPILOGUE

# The Challenge of the
# "Development of Doctrine"

Do the documents of the Second Vatican Council represent ends or beginnings? Are they self-contained; do they give the last word? Or are they marks of progress and developments of doctrine? Are they, in other words, open-ended? These questions are being discussed today with much fervor, because much of the success of the ecumenical movement is directly related to these questions.

Some leading theologians, and some members of the Curia in Rome, insist that these documents of the Second Vatican Council are the official teaching of the Roman Catholic Church and are therefore to be accepted without question. Other theologians, of equal standing, look upon these documents as the highest form of teaching of the Church *up to this time,* but they believe the documents themselves represent a "development of doctrine," and are therefore by their very nature open to examination and to further development.

The spirit of the Second Vatican Council seems to favor the latter interpretation—that of development. This being so, the next few years should be ones of real excitement and adventure under the leading of the Holy Spirit. Not only will Roman Catholic scholars begin looking forward to Vatican III, in which the Church will bring its teachings further up-to-date, but the rank and file of Church members will press forward into new and higher realms of thinking and action as members of the pilgrim Church.

This conception of the development of doctrine should also be congenial to Protestant churches since, as heirs of the Protestant Reformation, they view Christianity as being continually in the area of reform and renewal. Protestantism, which has lost some of its original motivation and questing, will now be challenged to look at itself again and to discover whether or not it truly represents the living truths of the Church of the New Testament. Protestantism, therefore, is challenged as much by these documents of Vatican II as are Roman Catholics. And if they do not continue to reform and renew themselves—their doctrines as well as their institutions—they may discover much to their surprise that they are no longer creative Protestants and radical leaders in the realistic application of the gospel to the daily life of the twentieth century.

The challenge of the Spirit of Truth today is making strong demands upon all branches of the Christian faith. Insofar as each of these great bodies of the Christian religion accepts the leadership of the Spirit of Truth honestly and fearlessly, the closer they will be drawn together. The ecumenical movement has much promise if within it are those who will accept the new revelation of God's truth, and will proceed to reconstruct doctrines and institutions on what they believe is God's will for the Church today and tomorrow. Christians have already come much closer together through open and frank dialogue; now may they proceed to follow their new friendly relationships with much more ecumenical action.

# *Appendices*

# I. The United Nations Declaration on Human Rights

## PREAMBLE

Whereas the recognition of the inherent dignity and of the equal and inalienable rights of all members of the human family is the foundation of freedom, justice and peace in the world;

Whereas, disregard and contempt for human rights have resulted in barbarous acts which have outraged the conscience of mankind, and the advent of a world in which human beings shall enjoy freedom of speech and belief and freedom from fear and want has been proclaimed as the highest aspiration of the common people;

Whereas it is essential, if man is not to be compelled to have recourse as a last resort to rebellion against tyranny and oppression, that human rights should be protected by the rule of law;

Whereas it is essential to promote the development of friendly relations between nations;

Whereas the peoples of the United Nations have in a charter reaffirmed their faith in fundamental human rights, in the dignity and worth of the human person and in the equal rights of men and women and have determined to promote social progress and better standards of life in a larger freedom;

Whereas the member states have pledged themselves to achieve in cooperation with the United Nations the promotion of universal respect for and observance of human rights and fundamental freedoms;

Whereas a common understanding of these rights and freedoms is of the greatest importance for full realization of this pledge,

Now therefore

The General Assembly

Proclaims this universal declaration of human rights as a common standard of achievement for all peoples and all nations, to the end that every individual and every organ of society keeping this declaration constantly in mind shall strive by teaching and education to promote respect for these rights and freedoms and by progressive measures, national and international, to secure their universal and effective recognition and observance, both among the peoples of the member states themselves and among the peoples of territories under their jurisdiction.

**ARTICLE 1.** All human beings are born free and equal in dignity and rights. They, endowed with reason and conscience, should act toward one another in a spirit of brotherhood.

**ARTICLE 2.** Everyone is entitled to all the rights and freedoms set forth in this declaration without distinction of any kind such as race, color, sex, language, religion, political or other opinion, national or social origin, property, birth, or other status.

Furthermore, no distinction shall be made on the basis of the political, jurisdictional or international status of the country or territory to which the person belongs, whether it be an independent, trust or non-self-governing territory or under any other limitation of sovereignty.

**ARTICLE 3.** Everyone has the right to life, liberty and security of person.

**ARTICLE 4.** No one shall be held in slavery or servitude; slavery and the slave trade shall be prohibited in all their forms.

**ARTICLE 5.** No one shall be subjected to torture or to cruel, inhuman or degrading treatment or punishment.

**ARTICLE 6.** Everyone has the right to recognition everywhere as a person before the law.

**ARTICLE 7.** All are equal before the law and are entitled without any discrimination to equal protection of the law. All are entitled to equal protection against any discrimination in violation of this declaration and against any incitement to such discrimination.

**ARTICLE 8.** Everyone has the right to effective remedy by competent national tribunals for acts violating fundamental rights granted him by a constitution or by-law.

**ARTICLE 9.** No one shall be subjected to arbitrary arrest, detention, or exile.

**ARTICLE 10.** Everyone is entitled in full equality to a fair and public hearing by an independent and impartial tribunal in the determination of his rights and obligations and of any criminal charge against him.

**ARTICLE 11.** 1. Everyone charged with a penal offense has the right to be presumed innocent until proved guilty according to law in a public trial at which he has had all guarantees necessary for his defense.

2. No one shall be held guilty of any penal offense on account of any act or omission which did not constitute a penal offense under national or international law at the time when it was committed. Nor shall a heavier penalty be imposed than one that was applicable at the time the penal offense was committed.

**ARTICLE 12.** No one shall be subjected to arbitrary interference with his privacy, family, home or correspondence nor to attacks upon his honor and reputation. Everyone has the right to the protection of the law against such interference or attacks.

**ARTICLE 13.** 1. Everyone has the right to freedom of movement and residence within the borders of each state.

2. Everyone has the right to leave any country, including his own, and to return to his country.

**ARTICLE 14.** 1. Everyone has the right to seek and to enjoy in other countries asylum from persecution.

2. This right may not be invoked in the case of prosecutions genuinely arising from non-political crimes or from acts contrary to the purposes and principles of the United Nations.

**ARTICLE 15.** 1. Everyone has the right to a nationality.

2. No one shall be arbitrarily deprived of his nationality nor denied the right to change his nationality.

**ARTICLE 16.** 1. Men and women of full age, without any limitation due to race, nationality or religion, have the right to marry and to found a family. They are entitled to equal rights as to marriage, during marriage and at its dissolution.

2. Marriage shall be entered into only with the free and full consent of the intending spouses.

3. The family is the natural and fundamental group

unit of society and is entitled to protection by society and the state.

**ARTICLE 17.** 1. Everyone has the right to own property alone as well as in association with others.

2. No one shall be arbitrarily deprived of his property.

**ARTICLE 18.** Everyone has the right to freedom of thought, conscience and religion. This includes the freedom to change his religion or belief and the freedom either alone or in community with others and in public or private to manifest his religion or beliefs in teaching, practices, worship and observance.

**ARTICLE 19.** Everyone has the right to freedom of opinion and expression; this right includes freedom to hold opinions without interference and to seek, receive and impart information and ideas through any media and regardless of frontiers.

**ARTICLE 20.** 1. Everyone has the right to freedom of peaceful assembly and association.

2. No one may be compelled to belong to an association.

**ARTICLE 21.** 1. Everyone has the right to take part in the government of his country, directly or through freely chosen representatives.

2. Everyone has the right of equal access to the public service in his country.

3. The will of the people shall be the basis of the authority of government; this will shall be expressed in periodic and genuine elections which shall be by universal and equal suffrage and shall be held by secret vote or by equivalent free voting procedures.

**ARTICLE 22.** Everyone, as a member of society, has the right to social security and is entitled to the realization through national effort and international co-operation and in accordance with the organization and resources of each state of the economic, social and cultural rights indispensable for his dignity and the free development of his personality.

**ARTICLE 23.** 1. Everyone has the right to work, to the free choice of employment, to just and favorable conditions of work and to protection against unemployment.

2. Everyone, without any discrimination, has the right to equal pay for equal work.

3. Everyone who works has the right to just and favorable remuneration insuring for himself and his family an

existence worthy of human dignity and supplemented, if necessary, by other means of social protection.

4. Everyone has the right to form and to join trade unions for the protection of his interests.

**ARTICLE 24.** Everyone has the right to rest and leisure, including reasonable limitation of working hours and periodic holidays with pay.

**ARTICLE 25.** 1. Everyone has the right to a standard of living adequate for the health and well-being of himself and his family, including food, clothing, housing and medical care and necessary social services and rights to security in the event of unemployment, sickness, disability, widowhood, old age or other lack of livelihood in circumstances beyond his control.

2. Motherhood and childhood are entitled to special care and assistance. All children, whether born in or out of wedlock, shall enjoy the same social protection.

**ARTICLE 26.** 1. Everyone has the right to education. Education shall be free, at least in the elementary and fundamental stages. Elementary education shall be compulsory. Technical and professional education shall be made generally available. Higher education shall be equally accessible to all on the basis of merit.

2. Education shall be directed to the full development of human personality and to the strengthening of respect for human rights and fundamental freedoms. It shall promote understanding, tolerance and friendship among all nations and racial or religious groups and shall further the activities of the United Nations for the maintenance of peace.

3. Parents have the prior right to choose the kind of education that shall be given to their children.

**ARTICLE 27.** 1. Everyone has the right freely to participate in the cultural life of the community, to enjoy the arts and to share in scientific advancement and its benefits.

2. Everyone has the right to the protection of the moral and material interests resulting from any scientific, literary, or artistic production of which he is the author.

**ARTICLE 28.** Everyone is entitled to a social and international order in which the rights and freedoms set forth in this declaration can be fully realized.

**ARTICLE 29.** 1. Everyone has duties to the community, in which alone the free, full development of his personality is possible.

2. In the exercise of his rights and freedoms, everyone shall be subject only to such limitations as are determined by law solely for the purpose of securing due recognition and respect for the rights and freedoms of others and of meeting the just requirements of morality, public order and the general welfare in a democratic society.

3. These rights and freedoms may in no case be exercised contrary to the purposes and principles of the United Nations.

**ARTICLE 30.** Nothing in this declaration may be interpreted as implying for any state, group or person any right to engage in any activity or to perform any act aimed at the destruction of any rights and freedoms set forth herein.

# II. The United States Bishops' Interim Guidelines for Prayer in Common and COMMUNICATIO IN SACRIS

The Decree on Ecumenism of the Second Vatican Council speaks of change of heart, holiness of life, and prayer for unity as the "soul" of the ecumenical movement (Ch. II, 8). The Bishops' Commission for Ecumenical Affairs, while taking steps to engage in dialogue and common action with the representatives of other churches, realizes that the question of prayer in common and *communicatio in sacris* is the most pressing of its tasks.

In presenting recommendations for common worship and prayer the Bishops' Commission recognizes that it is the local bishop who has the authority to make dispositions in this matter. The Secretariat for the Promotion of Christian Unity will, in time, present a directory for the practice of ecumenism which will be applicable throughout the universal Church. In the absence of such a directory and in the absence of legislation enacted by the Episcopal Conference of the United States, the Bishops' Commission for Ecumenical Affairs offers the following recommendations for the interim to the bishops of the United States.

## I. *Diocesan Ecumenical Commissions*

In guiding the course of ecumenism within their own dioceses, especially in presenting guidelines for prayer and *communicatio in sacris,* it is highly recommended that local bishops establish diocesan ecumenical commissions. Among the members of these commissions it would be desirable to include priests, religious and members of the laity who, by reason of their expert knowledge, can contribute to the work of the commissions, and who are also representative of the local churches. As the involvement of Catholics in dialogue, in joint action, and in prayer with other Christians increases such commissions could be of inestimable value to the local bishops.

In drawing up directives for *communicatio in sacris* and prayer in common it is also desirable to consult with other diocesan agencies, such as the Diocesan Liturgical Commission, and with leaders of the other churches of the community. The president and executive secretary of the local Council of Churches, for example, might be consulted before issuing regulations for the diocese.

## II.   *Prayer in Common between Catholics and Christians of Other Churches*

*Principles governing prayer in common, drawn from the Decree on Ecumenism, Chapter II, 8:*

"This change of heart and holiness of life, along with public and private prayer for the unity of Christians, should be regarded as the soul of the whole ecumenical movement, and merits the name, 'spiritual ecumenism.'

"It is a recognized custom for Catholics to meet for frequent recourse to that prayer for the unity of the Church with which the Saviour Himself on the eve of His death so fervently appealed to His Father: 'That they may all be one.' (Jn. 17, 20)

"In certain circumstances, such as in prayer services 'for unity' and during ecumenical gatherings, it is allowable, indeed desirable that Catholics should join in prayer with their separated brethren. Such prayers in common are certainly a very effective means of petitioning for the grace of unity, and they are a genuine expression of the ties which still bind Catholics to their separated brethren. 'For where two or three are gathered together in my name, there am I in the midst of them.' " (Mt. 18, 20)

In accordance with Section 8 of the Decree on Ecumenism the participation of Catholics with other Christians in services which are not part of the official liturgies of any communion, if these services are devoted to the cause of Christian unity, is highly desirable. Such services could fittingly be called "Ecumenical Services." Participation of Catholics in such services, whether they are held for the sake of promoting Christian unity in accordance with the Decree or, in the spirit of the Decree, for some other purpose, e.g., for peace, in time of public need, mourning, thanksgiving, etc., remains under the guidance of the local bishop.

The place chosen for the conduct of these ecumenical services should provide a worthy setting which is acceptable to all the participants and which, according to the prudent decision of the local bishop, is considered suitable.

With the approval of the local bishop, priests are to be encouraged to take an active part in the conduct of services, e.g. by reading Scripture lessons, preaching homilies, offering prayers and giving blessings.

The vesture to be worn at such services is also to be determined by the local bishop. In some circumstances ordinary civil attire may be the only appropriate form of dress for the participating priest. In other circumstances, since it is in accordance with Catholic usage even in the conduct of nonliturgical services, the use of the cassock and surplice may be considered. Another form of dress which is neither liturgical nor merely civil, namely, the use of the ferraiuola, may also be desirable on certain occasions. The value of some kind of "sacred" vesture is not to be underestimated in creating the right atmosphere for prayer in common. In reaching decisions concerning ecclesiastical vesture on these occasions it is highly recommended that there be consultation with the clergy of the other church bodies which are to participate in such services.

On occasion members of the Catholic laity may also be invited to take an active part in Ecumenical Services. They may, for example, be called upon to read the Scripture lessons. Under the guidance of the local bishop, who may well wish to consult his ecumenical commission regarding the qualifications of the laity invited to take these leading roles, such participation on the part of laymen has much to recommend it. The acceptance of such a policy could become one more manifestation of the Church's doctrine on the laity as found in the Constitution on the Church.

In preparing for and conducting these Ecumenical Services the principle of "reciprocity" should be kept in mind: to accept an invitation may often seem to entail an obligation to extend a similar invitation and to proffer an invitation may imply a readiness to receive one; one should not, therefore, accept an invitation if, according to Catholic norms, one cannot proffer a similar invitation.

All such joint services of prayer should be carefully prepared in accordance with the principle of "collaboration." The leaders of the participating groups should, after careful consideration, agree on the format of the services and on the choice of themes, Scripture readings and hymns. Prayers and hymns and homilies which may be unacceptable either to Catholics or to other Christians are to be avoided.

These Ecumenical Services, it is hoped, will complement the programs of prayer for unity which continue in our churches.

## III.  *Communicatio in Sacris*
*Principles governing communicatio in sacris:*

"Yet worship in common *(communicatio in sacris)* is not to be considered as a means to be used indiscriminately for the restoration of unity among Christians. There are two main principles upon which the practice of such common worship depends: first, that of the unity of the Church which ought to be expressed; and second, that of the sharing in means of grace. The expression of unity for the most part forbids common worship. Grace to be obtained sometimes commends it. The concrete course to be adopted, when due regard has been given to all the circumstances of time, place and persons, is left to the prudent decision of the local episcopal authority, unless the Bishops' Conference according to its own statutes, or the Holy See, has determined otherwise."—The Decree on Ecumenism, Chapter II, 8.

1) *Participation of Christians of Other Churches in the Liturgy of the Catholic Church*

Christians of other communions should be made welcome in attending Catholic liturgical celebrations. It is recommended, however, that great care be taken in issuing general invitations. The sensibilities of other ecclesial communities on proselytizing should also be respected in extending such invitations. It would be well to consult with leaders of other churches in formulating them. It is also worthy of note that general invitations may evoke invitations of a similar nature from other church bodies.

*Baptism and Confirmation:* From the nature of the office of sponsor, Christians of other communions may not be invited to act as sponsors at Baptism and Confirmation. The sponsor does not act only as a friend of the family nor only as one who promises to provide for the Christian education of the person to be baptized or confirmed, but also as a representative of the community of the Catholic faithful. As a representative of the community the sponsor stands as guarantor of the faith of the candidate he presents. A Christian not of our communion cannot be asked to assume this role.

*Holy Eucharist:* The Eucharist is the sign and at the same time is the cause of the unity of the Church. The restoration of Eucharistic Communion is the goal of our ecumenical effort. At the present time, however, except in particular cases of members of the Eastern Orthodox Church intercommunion with Christians of other denominations should not be permitted (cf. Decree on the Catholic Churches of the Eastern Rite, 26-29; Decree on Ecumenism, Ch. III, 15). Our separation is most keenly felt at the Table of the Lord, and the sense of sorrow awakened by a deepening realization of the meaning of this tragic separation should in itself provide a powerful stimulus to ecumenical concern among our people.

When, however, Christians of other communions are present at the Sacrifice of the Mass in our churches they may be invited to join, if they so desire, in the dialogue, in the recitation of prayers and in the singing of hymns. Christians of other churches may not, however, be invited to assume roles of leadership within the assembly, e.g., that of lector.

One of the great achievements of the Second Vatican Council is the Constitution on the Sacred Liturgy, and one of the most important emphases found in this document is that concerning the homily of the Mass (cf. Article 52). The homily is an integral part of the Liturgy and normally will be given by the celebrating bishop or priest. In breaking the bread of doctrine the homilist speaks on behalf of the local bishop and, in a sense, on behalf of the entire episcopal college. A clergyman of another communion cannot be asked to accept such a role.

Following the example of the liturgy of Good Friday it is recommended that public prayers for Christians of other communions be admitted within the liturgical celebrations. It is recommended, for example, that, when the presiding priest judges it appropriate, the names and intentions of

Christians of other communions be included within the *Prayer of the Faithful.*

*Holy Orders:* In the conferral of Holy Orders Christians of other communions must not be invited to take active roles. For reasons of friendship or courtesy, however, they may be invited to be present.

*Matrimony:* Christians of other churches may be admitted as witnesses and attendants at the celebration of Matrimony within the Catholic Church.

For the celebration of marriage between Catholics and Christians of other communions it is highly recommended that sacred rites be used according to the *Collectio Rituum* of 1964 and that the officiating priest be vested in cassock, surplice and stole.

Clergymen of other communions should not be invited to take an active role in the ceremony.

*Funerals:* It is recommended that, when requested by the family of the deceased, priests be permitted to conduct funeral services and to lead prayers at wakes for those not of our Church. It is for the local bishop to determine what rites are to be used on these occasions. In such circumstances burial in Catholic cemeteries may be permitted to those not of our communion, especially to spouses and relatives of Catholics. On the occasion of burials in Catholic cemeteries of those who were not Catholics it is also recommended that clergymen of other churches be permitted to conduct graveside services.

*Sacramentals:* The sacramentals of the Church may be given to those not of our communion who desire to receive them.

2) *Participation of Catholics in the Official Worship of Other Churches*

The Decree on Ecumenism does envisage *communicatio in sacris,* i.e., the participation of Catholics, under the supervision of the local bishop, in the liturgy of other communions (cf. Chapter II, 8). Catholics may attend official services of other churches which have special civic or social significance especially weddings and funerals. It should be remembered, however, that the Decree on Ecumenism makes repeated recommendations for caution and states that "worship in common (*communicatio in sacris*) is not to be considered as a means to be used indiscriminately for the restoration of unity among Christians."

*Baptism and Confirmation:* Catholics may not act as

sponsors at the conferral of Baptism or Confirmation in churches not of our communion; for reasons of friendship or courtesy, however, they may be present at these ceremonies.

*Holy Eucharist:* Catholics, accepting Eucharistic separation from their brothers of other churches in a penitential spirit and bearing in mind the principles mentioned above concerning the restoration of Eucharistic Communion, may not participate in the Eucharistic celebrations of other churches. For reasons of friendship or courtesy, however, they may be present at these services.

Catholic priests, remembering the Church's view regarding the homily at Holy Mass, may not accept invitations to preach during the Eucharistic celebrations of other churches.

*Holy Orders:* Catholics may not take an active role in the ordination ceremonies of other churches. Invitations to be present for these ceremonies, with the approval of the local bishop, may be accepted for reasons of friendship or courtesy.

*Matrimony:* Catholics, under the guidance of the local bishop, may be permitted to serve as witnesses at marriages which are celebrated in churches of other communions.

\* \* \* \*

Catholics should be mindful that attendance at services in other churches is not a substitution for, nor fulfillment of, their obligation to participate in the celebration of Holy Mass on Sundays and days of precept.

IV. *Communicatio in Sacris and Relations with the Eastern Orthodox Church*

With regard to *communicatio in sacris* with the Eastern Orthodox Church, the Decree on Ecumenism, Ch. III, 15, reads: "These Churches, although separated from us, yet possess true sacraments, above all—by apostolic succession —the priesthood and the Eucharist, whereby they are still joined to us in closest intimacy. Therefore some worship in common *(communicatio in sacris),* given suitable circumstances and the approval of church authority, is not merely possible but is encouraged."

The Decree on the Catholic Churches of the Eastern Rite (cf. Articles 26-29) established a new "conciliatory policy with regard to *communicatio in sacris* with the brethren of the separated Eastern Churches." Article 29 places the supervision of this policy in the care and control of local bishops. It encourages combined consultation on the part of these bishops and, if need be, consultation with the bishops of the Orthodox Churches.

The fulfillment of these articles is a matter of the utmost delicacy and the members of the Bishops' Commission for Ecumenical Affairs agree that there should be consultation concerning this matter with the ecclesiastical authorities of the Orthodox Churches. A subcommission has been established by the Bishops' Commission under the chairmanship of the Most Reverend Bernard J. Flanagan, Bishop of Worcester, and it will be among the tasks of this subcommission to explore, together with representatives appointed by the bishops of the Orthodox Church, this difficult question of *communicatio in sacris*.

V.   Throughout this statement of recommendations, it should be noted, frequent reference has been made to the role of the local bishop in guiding the practice of ecumenism but also with the spirit of the Constitution on the of the Bishops' Commission for Ecumenical Affairs are convinced, in accord not only with the Decree on Ecumenism but also with the spirit of the Constitution on the Church (Chapter III, 25-27) and the Constitution on the Sacred Liturgy. (Chapter I, 22, 41-42)

The unity of the Church is a "sacred mystery" and "the highest exemplar and source of this mystery is the unity, in the Trinity of Persons, of one God, the Father and the Son in the Holy Spirit." (Decree on Ecumenism, Ch. I, 2) In offering these recommendations the members of the Bishops' Commission for Ecumenical Affairs are guided by this vision of unity as a "mystery" and consequently share a conviction that Catholic participation in ecumenism must move beyond dialogue, programs of education, and cooperation in social matters to "spiritual ecumenism."

The renewal of the Church, and especially of the sacred liturgy, which is the concern of the Second Vatican Council, will, it is hoped, prepare our people for participation in the ecumenical movement and for prayer in common with other Christians. It is confidently expected that the annual observance of the Week of Prayer for Christian Unity, together with other programs of prayer, following the spirit of the renewed liturgy, will be extended and intensified in our churches. Our confidence in the efficacy of such prayer is based on the words of Our Lord, "For where two or three are gathered together in my name, there am I in the midst of them." (Mt. 18, 20)

At the first Eucharist, in the moments which preceded His passion and death, the Lord addressed Himself to His Father in His priestly prayer for unity. This prayer of Christ has become the prayer of the Church not only when these words are read and listened to, but above all, when the Church celebrates the Eucharist. While the pilgrim Church awaits the return of the risen Christ and the final consummation of all things in Him, the Eucharist remains the great sign and cause of the mysterious unity of the Church, and it is hoped that the Holy Sacrifice will be offered frequently for the cause of Christian unity.

In all of these endeavors which we describe as ecumenical—in dialogue, in giving common witness to the world, and in common prayer—we find the assurance we seek and require in the words of Christ's prayer: "that they all may be one; even as thou, Father, art in me, and I in thee, that they also may be one in us, so that the world may believe that thou hast sent me." (Jn. 17, 21)

# III. Guidelines for the Orthodox in Ecumenical Relations

*Published by the Standing Conference of Canonical Orthodox Bishops in America and commended to the clergy for guidance.*

*Written by* **The Reverend Leonidas Contos**

## INTRODUCTION

Whatever else may be written about the century in which we live, history will regard as one of its dominant themes the "ecumenical movement." It will record that Christianity exhausted its centrifugal forces which brought about its divisions and set out in an earnest quest for its lost unity. The seeds of disunity of course existed even in the New Testament Church. St. Paul writes with sorrow to the Corinthian Church about the divided loyalties of its members and asks in dismay, "Is Christ divided . . . ?" (I Cor. 1:11-13)

It is central to our faith that Christ is not divided; and this conviction has led modern theology increasingly to the corollary conviction that, whatever the appearance of things, the Church cannot be divided since it is the body of Christ. In spite of its very obvious divisions it is one, though with a oneness that we may not always, or readily, apprehend.

We recall Jesus asking ". . . that they may be one, as we are one." (John 17:21) And as it is not given us fully to know the nature of that inner oneness of Father and Son, so we may not fully comprehend the nature of the Church's inner oneness. As a Russian Orthodox layman expressed it more than a century ago, perhaps we are bound together "by ties which God has not yet willed to reveal to us."

This then is the essence of the ecumenical movement, a desire to know God's will for His Church. It is undertaken in faith, in obedience, and with a willingness to respond affirmatively to the urgings of the Holy Spirit. And the ecumenical vocation is addressed to the Orthodox Church no less than to the others, for though we know where the Church is, as a modern Orthodox thinker has put it, we cannot be sure where the Church is not.

Prayer for unity has long been a part of our Orthodox worship. But the familiar petition for the churches, "kai tis ton panton enoseos," has now ceased to be a hollow sentiment. Responding to initiatives taken by the Ecumenical Patriarchate nearly half a century ago, the Orthodox bodies are now wholly committed to a full and active role in this movement.

The pace of the movement has so quickened, especially as a consequence of historic changes now occurring within the Roman Catholic Church, that it is only natural that questions should arise in the minds of the faithful, both the clergy and the laity, as to what our engagement means. The Standing Conference has undertaken the preparation of this booklet in response to these questions, and to provide guidance to the priests as they become increasingly involved in "local ecumenicity." It is hoped that these pages will be ample enough to anticipate all likely questions, yet summary enough to be a convenient guide.

ARCHBISHOP IAKOVOS, President
The Standing Conference of Canonical Orthodox Bishops in America

# PART ONE

# THE ECUMENICAL MOVEMENT IN BRIEF OUTLINE

The conciliar movement of our time has grown naturally out of the activity of the Christian Community, principally of the Protestant tradition, in the various fields of social concern. The nineteenth century saw the formation of numerous volunteer associations in which Christians organized to make common cause in such matters as peace, temperance, and the like. The YMCA and the YWCA and the American and British Bible Societies are typical of this kind of movement.

Early in this century the separate missionary boards of various Church bodies, both in North America and Western Europe, began to sense the need for expressing Christian solidarity in their efforts. This led to a conference in Edinburgh in 1910, out of which grew the International Missionary Council; subsequent meetings (Jerusalem, 1925; Madras, 1938) carried the movement further.

In 1927 in Lausanne, Switzerland, a worldwide conference on the faith and order of the Churches was held for the first time. This and later conferences on Faith and Order (Edinburgh, 1937; Lund, Sweden, 1952; Montreal, 1963) became landmarks of the ecumenical movement.

Simultaneously a parallel stream of concern developed for the life and work of the Churches, with conferences taking place at Stockholm, 1925, and Oxford, 1937.

Shortly after the war, in 1948 at Amsterdam, these two movements, "Faith and Order" and "Life and Work," combined to form a new worldwide ecumenical body, the World Council of Churches. A second assembly of the

World Council was held in Evanston in 1954; the third at New Delhi in 1961, at which time the International Missionary Council was integrated into the World Council.

Often overlooked in the chronicles of modern ecumenicity is the fact that the Ecumenical Patriarchate very early took important initiatives toward the realization of Christian unity. In the historic encyclical of 1920, addressed to "All the Churches of Christ Wheresoever They Be," the Holy Synod of the Patriarchate urged the formation of a kind of League of Churches to be patterned after the then promising League of Nations. And while in that period of reconstruction after the "Great War" the Churches were otherwise preoccupied, nevertheless the significance of that great letter was not lost on the early ecumenical pioneers. Often startlingly contemporary in its grasp of the great social problems of our time, even though written nearly half a century ago, it remains today one of the most important of the ecumenical documents. For the sake of history, but as an insight to the Orthodox Church's profound commitment to and comprehension of the cause of unity, it is reproduced here in translation.

# THE PATRIARCHAL ENCYCLICAL OF 1920—UNTO ALL THE CHURCHES OF CHRIST WHERESOEVER THEY BE

*"See that ye love one another with a pure heart fervently."* (I Peter 1:22)

Our Church is persuaded that a closer relationship and a mutual understanding among the several Christian Churches is not hindered by their doctrinal differences; that such understanding is both desirable and necessary, indeed in the best interests of the Churches, both individually and as the whole Body of Christ; that it will prepare and facilitate that perfect blessed union which, with God's help, may one day be realized.

Our Church regards the present time as a most propitious to bring this important question forward for common study. For while ancient prejudices, traditions, pretensions even, which have in the past frustrated the work of unity may even now raise difficulties, nevertheless, it is better to face those difficulties; if there be good will and good intent, they neither can nor ought to prove insuperable obstacles.

Thus, with the establishment of the League of Nations, holding such high promise, we consider the question of unity even more feasible and timely; and so, filled with hope, we beg leave to make this summary statement of our thoughts and conviction, addressing it both to our other brothers in the East and the venerable Christian Churches of the West wheresoever they be.

It is our view that two things can best contribute to bring us into such desirable and beneficial intercourse, to achieve it and publicly to manifest it:

First of all we deem it necessary and indispensable to remove all mutual distrust and friction between the various Churches, resulting from the tendency, unfortunately common with some, to entice and convert followers of other confessions. For one cannot ignore what is taking place even now, disturbing the internal peace of the Churches, especially those of the East, to whose trials and afflictions their own brethren thus add. And when measured against the trifling results of such proselytizing, how great is the resentment and hostility that it produces!

With sincerity and mutual confidence thus restored among the Churches, we believe that charity, too, must be revived and deepened, so that they will no longer regard one another as strangers, enemies even, but as relatives and friends in Christ, "fellow heirs, members of the same body, and partakers of the promise in Christ Jesus through the gospel." (Eph. 3:6) And when the several Churches are inspired by love, placing it above all else in their judgment of one another and in their relations to one another, they will then be able to lessen rather than increase and widen the differences that divide them. By promoting a constant brotherly concern for the conditions, the stability and the wellbeing of the other Churches; by their eagerness to know what is happening in those Churches and by acquiring a more accurate knowledge of them; by their readiness, whenever the occasion arises, to offer the helping hand; they will accomplish much good, to their own credit and profit and that of the whole Christian body, and to the furtherance of the cause of unity.

This friendship and charitable intent toward one another can, in our view, be demonstrated and articulated in certain specific ways: 1.) By the acceptance of a uniform calendar for the simultaneous celebration of the great Christian festivals by all the Churches; 2.) by the exchange of fraternal letters, when it is customary, on the great feasts of the ecclesiastic year and other special occasions; 3.) by more cordial relations between representatives of the various Churches wherever they may be; 4.) by exchanges between theological schools and prominent theologians, as well as the students of various denominational seminaries; 5.) by convening Pan-Christian conferences to examine questions of common interest to all the Churches; 6.) by the impartial investigation, historically valid, of doctrinal differences, both from the professorial chair and in scholarly writings; 7.) by mutual respect of the customs and usages common to each Church; 8.) by allowing to one another the use of chapels and cemeteries for funerals and interment of persons of other confessions dying in foreign lands; 9.) by settling the question of inter-confessional marriages, and finally, 10.) by mutual support of one another in the work of undergirding religious faith, the work of charity, and every such common task.

Such open and vital intercourse between the Churches will the more greatly benefit the whole body of the Church; for today's dangers no longer threaten a particular Church but all of them together, attacking as they do the very foundations of Christian faith and the very composition of Christian life and society. The terrible war that has just ended has thrown light onto the inner life of the Christian nations and disclosed many unhealthy signs, a profound disrespect for the basic principles of justice and humanity; it has not only aggravated old wounds, but opened new ones of more pressing nature to which the Churches need to give great attention and care.

Alcoholism, daily gaining ground; superfluous luxury on the increase, under the pretext of making life more beautiful and pleasurable; voluptuousness and lust thinly veiled under the cloak of freedom and emancipation of the body; gross license and indecency in literature, painting, the theatre, and in music, posing respectably as good taste and sophistication in the fine arts; the deification of wealth with a corollary contempt for the higher ideals—all these things present the gravest danger to the constitution of Christian society. These are the questions of the day, and they call for common study and cooperation on the part of the Christian Churches.

Finally, it is the duty of the Churches, graced with the sacred name of Christ, no longer to forget and neglect His "new commandment," the great mandate of love; no longer to trail piteously behind the political leaders who, in the true spirit of the Gospel of Christ and the justice of Christ, have already instituted with auspicious beginnings the League of Nations, for the defense of right and for the cultivation of love and harmony among the nations.

For all these reasons, and in the hope that the other Churches will share the thoughts and convictions we have here set forth on the urgency of promoting, at least as a beginning, such cooperation and intercourse among the Christians, we request each one to make known to us in reply its own thoughts and beliefs concerning this matter. Once we have by consensus and agreement defined the objective, we may safely proceed together toward its realization, and thus, "speaking the truth in love, we [may] grow up in every way into him who is the head, into Christ, from whom the whole body, joined and knit together by every joint with which it is supplied, when each part is working properly, makes bodily growth and upbuilds itself in love." (Eph. 4:15)

At the Patriarchate of Constantinople, in the month of January, the year of grace one thousand nine hundred and twenty.

The Locum Tenens of the Ecumenical Throne:

Metropolitan of Brussa, DOROTHEUS
Metropolitan of Caesarea, NICOLAOS
Metropolitan of Kyzicus, CONSTANTINOS
Metropolitan of Amassia, GERMANOS
Metropolitan of Pissidia, GERASIMOS
Metropolitan of Angora, GERVASIOS
Metropolitan of Ainos, JOACHIM
Metropolitan of Vizye, ANTHIMOS
Metropolitan of Silivria, EUGENIOS
Metropolitan of Saranta Ecclesiae, AGATHANGELOS

Metropolitan of Tyroloe and Serentium, CHRYSOSTO-
MOS

Metropolitan of the Dardanelles and Lampsacos,
IRINAIOS

---

In a May, 1964, Study Report of the World Council
of Churches, reference is made to the Patriarchal Synod's
Encyclical. It reads: "This letter was one of the major
factors leading to the foundation of the World Council
of Churches at Amsterdam in 1948."

## THE COUNCILS OF CHURCHES

THE WORLD COUNCIL OF CHURCHES, with
permanent headquarters at Geneva, is made up of more
than two hundred member churches from ninety-three
countries. Neither a church body nor a "super-church,"
it is rather a cooperative agency through which the member churches reflect their deeper sense of oneness by developing and maintaining common programs of ecumenical action, engaging in interchurch aid, service to refugees
and the like, and carrying on a broad program of study
through the Ecumenical Institute at Chateau de Bossey,
near Geneva.

THE NATIONAL COUNCIL OF THE CHURCHES
OF CHRIST in the United States is in most respects the
counterpart of the World Council, with thirty-one member
churches in the United States, eight of them Orthodox.
Through its various program boards and commissions, the
membership of which includes many Orthodox priests and
laymen, it carries on a wide spectrum of activity in behalf
of its member churches and their constituencies. A few
examples: migrant ministry; services to American Indians;
spiritual and welfare service in state institutions; film
production and distribution; radio and television broad-
casting; resettlement of refugees; development of curriculum for Sunday Schools; foreign student programs;
university campus work; services to local councils of
churches. The NCC is governed by its General Assembly
which meets every three years; responsibility for carrying
out its program and policies rests with the General Board,
meeting normally three times a year.

LOCAL AND STATE COUNCILS have existed in various forms for many years, ranging from local church federations to large and complex metropolitan councils with broad cooperative programs, to councils functioning on a statewide level. The common service and witness of local churches in local communities provides the real foundation for the whole ecumenical movement, and it is this reality that gives force to the statement of the New Delhi Assembly of the World Council (1961) which began: "We believe that the unity which is both God's will and his gift to his Church is being made visible *as all in each place* who are baptized into Jesus Christ and confess him as Lord and Savior are brought by the Holy Spirit into ONE fully committed fellowship. . . ."

## ORTHODOXY AND THE ECUMENICAL BODIES

We have already sketched the history of the Ecumenical Movement and have seen how earnestly the Orthodox Churches, especially those under the Ecumenical Patriarchate, have approached the great issues of Christian unity. At the New Delhi Assembly of the World Council of Churches, the Churches of Russia, Rumania and Bulgaria formally sought and were admitted to full membership in that body, a matter of far more than numerical significance.

Most of the national Orthodox Churches now have membership in the World Council, participating in the numerous commissions and committees through which it functions. The Ecumenical Patriarchate, as we have seen, has since 1954 had a permanent representative at its Geneva headquarters, currently in the person of Metropolitan Aimilianos Timiades. Archbishop Iakovos, the first to serve in that capacity as Metropolitan Melitis, is one of the Council's six presidents, as was Archbishop Michael before him, and the late Archbishops of Thyateira, Germanos and Athenagoras, formerly. Dr. Nikos Nissiotis, a Greek lay theologian, has been for some years associate director of the Ecumenical Institute, the World Council's great study center, at Bossey, near Geneva. He is soon to become its director.

Eight Orthodox jurisdictions in the United States now have full membership in the National Council of Churches.

Archbishop Iakovos serves as Vice President of that body, while a number of our Bishops, priests and laymen, from all jurisdictions, serve on its General Board and the larger General Assembly, as well as numerous commissions and program boards.

The Greek Archdiocese now maintains its Office of Interchurch Relations and Office of Communications at the Interchurch Center, 475 Riverside Drive, New York, where the National Council has its headquarters and several denominational offices are located.

# ORTHODOXY AND THE SEPARATED EASTERN CHURCHES

The earliest breach in Christendom came as a consequence of the Fourth Ecumenical Council at Chalcedon in 451. Both Chalcedon and an earlier Council, at Ephesus in 431, dealt with the complex christological controversies of that period. The Chalcedonian definition: that Jesus Christ was truly God and truly man, having two natures and two wills perfectly united, was ultimately rejected by large segments of the Church in the Middle East and North Africa. These Nestorian and Monophysite bodies, though sharing much of the tradition of Orthodoxy, are nevertheless not in communion with us.

In recent years the conviction has grown that these bodies remained in separation from the Byzantine Church largely as a consequence of political events in history, not the least of which was the rapid spread of Islam from the early seventh century. The natural affinity of these Churches, notably the Coptic and the Armenian, with the Orthodox has been more keenly sensed in recent times, and there has been a growing consensus that the christological differences may be less substantive than once thought, and more susceptible to re-interpretation.

The first step toward exploring the possibility of reunion among the Churches of the East was taken at Aarhus, in Denmark, in the summer of 1964, when theologians of both persuasions met in a highly amicable series of discussions and set the stage for a continuing dialogue.

# PART TWO

# BASIC PRINCIPLES OF ECUMENICITY

The Vatican Council's Decree on Ecumenism speaks in terms of "spiritual ecumenism." The term implies change of heart and renewal of the inner life as basic to the constant renewal of the Church; it also implies prayer for unity which begins by acknowledging the sin of disunity. It is a good term. For not only is the sin of pride a major cause of Christian divisions; it is always present to frustrate our best intentions of overcoming them.

"Spiritual ecumenism" likewise implies that in our relations to our brothers of other persuasions we must always presume their sincerity. This means in turn that we must accept their criticism of us as made in good faith, whether such criticism is valid or simply the product of misunderstanding. When others' attitudes seem to reflect a lack of knowledge, we should be willing patiently to explain our position, and just as patiently to learn from them. "Spiritual ecumenism" inevitably leads us to what might be called "intellectual, or intelligent, ecumenism," which is precisely what dialogue is.

But to engage profitably in dialogue, it is essential that we know the Orthodox position thoroughly. Dialogue cannot be carried on among the clergy alone. Local ecumenism, ultimately the only real ecumenism, must involve the people as well. Unhappily, we are likely to find our lay people inadequately prepared for such encounter; therefore it is urged that the parishes undertake a far more serious program of education, both in Orthodox faith and practice and in comparative religion, than has been the norm.

## LOCAL ECUMENICITY: PARTICIPATION IN:

**ECUMENICAL DIALOGUE.** The term dialogue means

nothing more nor less than Christian conversation, at least in the local and informal context. Love grows out of knowing one another; essential therefore to dialogue is the fullest possible knowledge and understanding of those with whom we are engaged in conversation. The priests bear a large responsibility in this regard, not only to be themselves well informed, and well disposed, but to minister to the laity in terms of guidance and enlightenment.

Even if the parish has no library—and surely every parish should, and can—the familiar tract rack can be substantially enriched in ecumenical literature of the kind designed to give the average layman a good working knowledge of other Christian traditions, about the ecumenical bodies, and of the history of the movement. The reading list appended to these guidelines may be helpful in this connection.

But it is equally imperative that the laity be well rooted in Orthodox faith and practices before they attempt to interpret them to others or defend them.

A careful distinction needs to be made between kinds of dialogue. What is meant here is informal conversation. It may involve the priest with clergy of the Roman Catholic and Protestant traditions; or it may bring lay people together in such encounters as "Living Room Dialogues," for which texts have been carefully developed with the approval of the Orthodox Church. In dialogue of this kind it must be clear that the individual, priest or layman, while speaking as an Orthodox, does not represent his Church or its position in any official way, unless designated to do so.

Those so designated are engaged in Dialogue properly so called, exploring with others, similarly equipped and designated, doctrines of faith, variances of tradition, and modes of Christian action as governed by faith and tradition.

No priest or layman may undertake to represent the Church officially without prior appointment or approval by his ecclesiastical head.

Whether it be Dialogue in this latter sense, or merely informal conversations, the principle of "parity" ought to apply. That is, participants should be relatively equal in number as well as in the level of their intellectual and spiritual maturity.

**ECUMENICAL ASSEMBLIES.** Ecumenical assemblies of various kinds have become increasingly popular and meaningful. Programs of formal dialogue such as panels, interfaith forums and convocations, open house programs, etc., are desirable ways of improving understanding across confessional lines. These are best arranged through local Councils of Churches or ministerial associations or existing interfaith committees.

To participate in any public assembly of this nature, beyond the purely local (in the case of large Metropolitan cities, neighborhood) level, the priest should advise his Bishop and be authorized by him beforehand. This also applies where the priest is invited to address such an assembly or, in an ecumenical setting, to preach the sermon. In all such instances the effort should be made to reflect the mind of the Church through the use of published sources of its theologians and leaders.

Basic to correct relations with clergy of other communions is the principle of reciprocity. Stated plainly this means that in extending an invitation one is prepared to receive one, and, conversely, accepting an invitation implies readiness to extend one. Generally speaking, if we are unable to reciprocate an invitation, we should not accept one. There are obvious exceptions to this, of course; but when in doubt it is best to consult the ecclesiastical authority. There is no problem when a priest is asked to address a church group in a parish hall or other suitable place other than a church. But to return the courtesy of the pulpit raises for us some delicate problems.


**ECUMENICAL WORSHIP.** When the Lord declares, "Where two or three are gathered in my name, there am I in the midst of them," (Matt. 18:20) there is no inference of fellowship only within confessional boundaries. So that when we join our otherwise separated brothers in common supplication, it is an expression of our being bound together by those "ties which God has not yet willed to reveal to us."

Ecumenical services properly so called are devotional services conducted for special reasons, most commonly for Christian Unity, especially during the Week of Prayer for Christian Unity in January; or for peace, or in time of public calamity, public mourning, public thanksgiving, etc.

When held in a neutral public place not usually reserved for formal worship, no special problems arise. But if held in a church, the service should be publicly recognized as "ecumenical" in character so as to avoid misunderstanding.

There are real difficulties here that ought honestly to be faced. And in facing them and identifying them, we can help make clear a basic Orthodox (and indeed Roman Catholic) position: that unity at the altar (communicatio in sacris) must be seen as the ultimate fruit of our labors and of our painful unity efforts, but not the means to that unity.

Permission must be obtained from the Bishop to hold services in Orthodox Churches to which clergy of other communions are to be invited. Such services would follow one of the accepted forms, i.e. Vespers, Matins, Compline, etc. Any accommodation as to the language of such service must likewise have previous sanction.

When participating in a service in a hall or public place, ordinary civil attire will usually be appropriate for an Orthodox priest. In other circumstances he will wear the rasson with pectoral cross (if so entitled), or academic dress when indicated. No part of eucharistic vesture, such as stole, is proper.

**LOCAL AND STATE COUNCILS.** As has been suggested earlier, the experience of sincere Christian people in the local community forms the soundest base for the whole ecumenical development. One of the primary benefits of the movement, even without that final unity for which Christ prayed, and for which we too pray and work, is the freedom of all Christian bodies to labor together for the general good of society. And such cooperation can be very vital and real at the local level, where the common problems and concerns are many: education, public welfare, racial tensions, urban renewal, unemployment. If "koinonia" in the fullest sense is difficult for us to realize, indeed even to define adequately, at this stage of our ecumenical maturity, yet "diakonia" can and should unite us.

The Councils of Churches, at the local level, are an appropriate and desirable means for achieving such cooperation. They represent a long tradition and rich experience in coordinating the activities of the Churches in the area of civic and social witness and service.

Where membership is in terms of local congregations, the priest should feel free to encourage his parish council into a working partnership. Normally the formula of financial participation is based on a percentage of the individual church's budget; however, such sharing is seen as a voluntary commitment. Since we tend to make limited use of Council resources—released time, chaplaincies, worship and arts commissions, planning departments, etc.—experience shows that the financial commitment is less important to a local Council.

When invited, Priests may accept positions on Boards of Directors. But they should also try to engage some of their most capable and ecumenically oriented laymen. Such election must be brought to the attention of the Bishop. Women's groups should be encouraged to have formal liaison with local units of United Church Women as well as with counterpart groups in the Roman Catholic community.

Ministerial Associations provide an excellent means for the Priest to know his colleagues and to understand their view better. Many such groups now extend fellowship to Roman Catholic priests, and often to members of the local rabbinate as well.

Relationships to State Councils present greater difficulties, principally because our jurisdictional subdivisions do not as a rule coincide with the geographical limits of such Councils. Thus membership as judicatories is not possible. However, when invited to work on program boards, or elected to office in a State Council, or large Metropolitan Council, a Priest may accept, but only with his Bishop's consent. Orthodox Councils of Clergy which correspond to the general area of a State Council may, when appropriate, accept membership as a group.

## QUESTIONS IN PARTICULAR

**INTERCOMMUNION.** As it has been stated in an earlier chapter, we accept with pain and sorrow the reality of our separation at the Lord's Table, while at the same time acknowledging His call to work and pray earnestly for that fulness of our unity in Him.

The Vatican Council's Decree on Ecumenism, when making reference to the Eastern Churches, envisages greater freedom of worship and intercommunication with the Orthodox, while recognizing that careful, and probably long, consultations with Eastern Catholic and Orthodox theologians must precede such a step.

The Standing Conference of Canonical Orthodox Bishops in America meanwhile has taken the clear position that the Orthodox faithful may not receive Communion outside their churches. The reverse of course is likewise generally true, that is, non-Orthodox may not receive Communion in an Orthodox Church.

**CHURCH ATTENDANCE.** Persons of other confessions are, of course, welcome to attend the Holy Eucharist and other services in Orthodox churches. Clergy of other communions attending Orthodox worship, whether the Divine Liturgy or other service, may be made welcome as guests of honor, and given some special place within the soleas. High dignitaries of other Churches, when the formal occasion indicates, might be seated adjacent to the Bishop's throne, when a Bishop is officiating.

Again the principle of reciprocity becomes operative, for these are matters in which others' sensibilities must be most thoughtfully respected. Invitations to groups from other traditions need to be addressed with particular care so that they do not appear to imply sacramental communion.

For purposes of acquiring a deeper knowledge and understanding of the beliefs and practices of others, our people may, when accompanied by their priest, attend official worship in other churches—especially as part of the regular Sunday School and Youth religious programs.

**PREACHING.** In its Constitution on the Sacred Liturgy Vatican II defines the homily as an integral part of the Liturgy, implying that "in breaking the bread of doctrine the homilist speaks on behalf of the local bishop" and, in a sense, of the entire hierarchy. In this light it is clear that a clergyman of another communion cannot be asked to assume such a role.

The Orthodox position, inferred from our whole tradition, and deriving from our fundamental concept of the Liturgy as the principal means of expressing the mystery of Christ and the real nature of the Church, is substantially the same. Given this position, the principle of reciprocity does not permit an Orthodox priest to accept an invitation to preach at an official eucharistic service of another communion. Obviously, exceptions to this rule may be possible, but only with the express permission of the Bishop.

**SACRAMENTS AND SACRAMENTALS.** Broadly speaking the attitude of the Roman Catholic Church is now more irenic and liberal with respect to the Sacraments; however, some uncertainty still prevails, and local practice occasionally varies, with particular regard to Baptism and Matrimony.

A Catholic Priest, in the spirit of the Decree on Ecumenism, should no longer confer conditional Baptism indiscriminately on those who have been previously baptized. Candidates validly baptized are received into the Church through the Profession of Faith alone. When made aware of violations of this position, involving Orthodox, our clergy ought, with great kindness, to call attention to the acknowledged validity of Orthodox Baptism.

When receiving into the Orthodox Church one who comes voluntarily from another discipline, the Priest will accept the candidate through one of the three modes prescribed by the Quinisext Ecumenical Council: baptism, chrismation or confession of faith, whichever is appropriate.

While they may be present at ceremonies involving friends or relatives, members of the Orthodox Church may not act as sponsors in Baptism or Confirmation in non-Orthodox Churches. Conversely, a member of another communion cannot be asked to assume the role of sponsor in Orthodox Baptism or Confirmation.

In some instances involving inter-confessional marriage, the Catholic Church now permits "dual" performance of the Sacrament of Matrimony: in the Catholic Church and in the church of the non-Catholic party. The Orthodox Church does not favor this practice; in every such instance the Priest must take particular care to receive prior permission from his Bishop.

Our people may participate as witnesses and attendants in marriage solemnized in other churches. Similarly members of other confessions may be permitted to act as attendants at Orthodox weddings; they may not, however, act as witnesses in the explicit sense of "paranymphos" or best man.

The Orthodox Church has long made provision in the Efhologion for burial of persons not of the Orthodox faith under certain conditions. However, this dispensation is not a general one and ought not to be misconstrued to cover too broad a range of circumstances. When in doubt the Priest should consult his Bishop.

There is now far greater leniency in the matter of interment of non-Catholics in Catholic cemeteries. At the request of the family of the deceased, priests and ministers of other communions normally are permitted to officiate at graveside services. Accordingly, Orthodox Priests may accede to such requests, wearing rasson and stole, and reading the customary Trisagion; but may not participate in funeral services as such in other churches.

# FOR FURTHER
# ECUMENICAL
# READING

*Authority in the Church*, John L. McKenzie, S.J., Sheed and Ward.

*Catholic Almanac, The* (annually), Doubleday and St. Anthony's Guild.

*Catholic Primer on the Ecumenical Movement, A*, Gustave Weigel, S.J., Newman (paperback).

*Catholic Quest for Christian Unity, The*, Gregory Baum, Paulist Press.

*Church After the Council, The*, Karl Rahner, Herder and Herder.

*Church Tomorrow, The*, George H. Tavard, Herder and Herder.

*Consultation On Church Union* (COCU), official reports of the four meetings of the Consultation, Foreword Movement Miniature.

*Council Daybook*, ed. by Floyd Anderson (4 sessions in 3 volumes), National Catholic Welfare Conference.

*Council in Action, The*, Hans Küng, Sheed and Ward.

*Council, Reform and Reunion, The*, Hans Küng, Sheed and Ward.

*Council Speeches of Vatican II*, ed. by Hans Küng, Yves Congar, O.P., Daniel O'Hanlon, S.J., Paulist Press.

*Current Trends in Theology*, edited by Donald J. Wolf, S.J., and James V. Schall, S.J., Doubleday (Image Book).

*Dialogue: Vatican II, The*, by correspondents of Religious News Service, published by the National Conference of Christians and Jews.

*Documents of Vatican II, The*, ed. by Walter M. Abbott,

S.J., Association Press, America Press, and Guild Press (paperback); Association Press and Herder and Herder (cloth).

*Ecumenical Experiences*, ed. by Louis V. Romeun, Burns and Oates, London.

*Ecumenism and Vatican II*, Charles O'Neill, S.J., Bruce.

*Edinburgh 1937*, Hugh Martin, SCM Press, London.

*English Bishops at the Council*, ed. by Derek Worlock, Burns and Oates, London (paperback).

*Evanston Report, The*, World Council of Churches, 1954, ed. by W. A. Visser't Hooft, Harper and Row.

*Faith and Order*, Proceedings of the World Conference, Lausanne, 1927, ed. by H. N. Bate, SCM Press, London.

*Freedom Today*, Hans Küng, Sheed and Ward.

*Historical Road of Eastern Orthodoxy*, Alexander Schmemann.

*Honesty in the Church*, Daniel Callahan, Scribner's.

*How We Got Our Denominations*, Stanley I. Stuber, Association Press.

*Institutionalism and Church Unity*, ed. by Nils Ehrenstrom and Walter G. Muelder, Association Press.

*John XXIII and the City of Man*, Peter Riga, Newman Press.

*Learning to Worship*, Theodor Filthant, Newman Press.

*Liturgy of Vatican II, The*, ed. by William Barauna, O.F.M., Franciscan Herald Press.

*Living Room Dialogues*, William B. Greenspun, C.S.P., and William A. Norgren, National Council of Churches and Paulist Press.

*Mind of the Catholic Layman, The*, Daniel Callahan, Scribner's.

*New Delhi Report, The*, World Council of Churches, 1961, ed. by W. A. Visser't Hooft, Association Press.

*New Reformation?*, John A. T. Robinson, Westminster Press (paperback).

*Observer in Rome*, Robert McAfee Brown, Doubleday.

*On the Road to Christian Unity*, Samuel McCrea Cavert, Harper and Row.

*Open Church, The*, Michael Novak, Macmillan.

*Orthodox Church, The*, John Meyendorff.

*Our Changing Liturgy*, C. J. McNaspy, S.J., Hawthorn.

*Outlines of the 16 Documents, Vatican II*, prepared by Virginia Mary Hefferman, The America Press.

*Oxford Conference, Official Report, The,* ed. by J. H. Oldham, Willett, Clark & Co.

*Primer on Roman Catholicism for Protestants,* Stanley I. Stuber, Association Press.

*Principles of Church Union* (adopted by the Consultation at its meeting in 1966), Forward Movement Miniature.

*Problem of Religious Freedom, The,* John Courtney Murray, S.J., Newman Press (paperback).

*Question of Mary, The,* Rene Laurentin, Holt, Rinehart and Winston.

*Religion and Society: The Ecumenical Impact,* Claud D. Nelson, Sheed and Ward.

*Religious Liberty,* Cecil Northcott, SCM Press, London.

*Social Thought of the World Council of Churches, The,* Edward Duff, S.J., Association Press.

*Stand on Ecumenism: The Council's Decree, A,* Lorenz Cardinal Jaeger, Kenedy.

*Steps to Christian Unity,* edited by John A. O'Brien, Collins (Fontana paperback).

*Third Session, The,* Xavier Rynne, Farrar, Straus and Company.

*Third World Conference on Faith and Order, The,* ed. by Oliver S. Tomkins, SCM Press.

*Travail of Religious Liberty, The,* Roland H. Bainton, Harper and Row (paperback).

*Twelve Council Fathers,* Walter M. Abbott, S.J., Macmillan.

*Unity in Freedom,* Augustin Cardinal Bea, Harper and Row.

*Vatican Council and All Christians, The,* Claud D. Nelson, Association Press.

*Vatican Council II, From John XXIII to Paul VI,* booklet, The America Press.

*Vatican Diary,* Douglas Horton, United Church Press.

*Vatican II: An Interfaith Appraisal,* ed. by John M. Miller, C.S.C., University of Notre Dame Press and Association Press.

*What Happened at Rome?,* Gary MacEoin, Holt, Rinehart and Winston.

# INDEX